SHORT STUFF
on the job with an x-small model

Isobella Jade

Buzz on Isobella Jade and her books

"A shade under 5-feet-4, Isobella Jade has been building a brand
— herself — for the petite model."
–The New York Daily News

"Before Tyra was giving shorties hope on Cycle 13 of
'America's Next Top Model,' Isobella Jade was already in their
corner."
–The Los Angeles Times

"Petite model Isobella Jade has faced some diversity in the
modeling world, to say the least….But she busted right through
those 'you're too short' obstacles to land modeling gigs for
Macy's, Victoria's Secret, and more."
–Glamour magazine

"Isobella Jade may seem an unlikely graphic novel writer,
coming from the modeling world. But then, she was an unlikely
model. Jade, standing about 5 feet, 4 inches tall, calls herself the
Seabiscuit of models, referring to the undersized thoroughbred
that became a racing sensation."
–Publishers Weekly

"It looks like we can welcome Isobella Jade to the ranks of those
writers who believed in themselves so fiercely that they attracted
the faith of others as well."
–GalleyCat, Media Bistro

"*Almost 5'4"* is a very readable, very revealing memoir that feels
at times like you are peeking at someone's secret diary."
–MacWorld UK

Gamine Press
ISBN-13: 9780615317434
ISBN: 061531743X

Cover graphic by Jazmin Ruotolo

CONTENTS

HEIGHT ISN'T EVERYTHING

MODELING TIPS FOR SHORT CHICKS

Give yourself a chance.

Whenever I shoot I inhale, stretch my torso and arch my back to get a few more inches. I lift my chin slightly, I stretch my legs and keep some space between my body and my arms to create length. I point my toes, watch my posture and stay aware of my proportions – I put it all to use to prove that I am just as good as any of those tall lanky giraffe models.

~ Isobella Jade on being a short model

Height isn't everything

I love it when the photographer or casting director looks all the way through my book (portfolio). I see it as a sign they like me and my chances for booking this job are good. Usually if they say *"Thank you for coming!"* in an enthusiastic tone it means I didn't book the job. And too much kindness from the photographer or casting director means they're really thinking I shouldn't have come or I'm not what we're looking for. Well, I have all these theories. But who really knows until the phone rings – or doesn't. Actually, these days my agents typically email me. Sometimes not even a full email, just something in the subject implying my urgent response based on the job or casting:

Subject: available Monday?

Subject: can you wear a 37 shoe?

Subject: avail tue-wed-fri next week?

Subject: confirm Thursday for Macy's shoot

Subject: shoot for Easy Spirit/Wednesday

Subject: hold Tuesday

Subject: NEED HAND DIGITALS ASAP

Subject: avail tomorrow?

Being available has definitely helped me book work.
I might not be the prettiest or the tallest, but by making the most of what I do have – nice hands, nice legs, nice feet, nice

skin, nice body – I have become one of the tiniest working models out there. Years of being in front the camera have taught me how to work my proportions to look longer and leaner and how to be more perfect for the job.

Sure, some days I get annoyed of it. Being judged for how long my fingernails are today, sometimes even having to stretch my thumb to make it appear longer. Or waiting to hear back about whether my smile or if my spunk is spunky enough and if it's what they are looking for. Or if my skin-tone is the right tone. Or if my foot fits the shoe well enough for the campaign. Or if the shape of my ass is what they are looking for. We can go on all day with the different scenarios.

But being judged and analyzed is the lifestyle of a model. And knowing that I've made myself a model from scratch and used what I do have to get ahead and get the job done keeps me motivated, inspired and chasing more. I am addicted to the rush of getting the chance.

You might have heard about my modeling memoir called *Almost 5'4"* which is about the grit and hustle I experienced to become a model. Here you will find what followed, some of my on-the-job moments modeling for national brands and magazines – times when an x-small model got the job done.

Isobella Jade

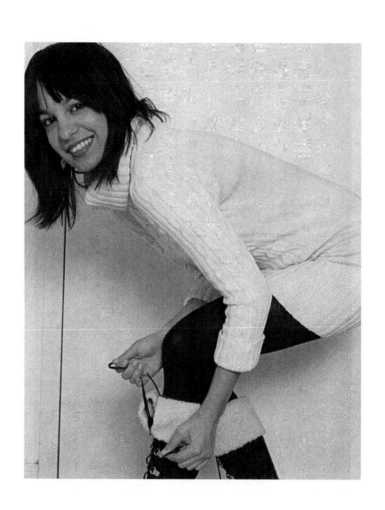

Subject: confirm tomorrow
you are Christina Ricci's body double for movie poster

It was a rainy Thursday evening and I received a last minute booking request thanks to my tiny size. I was told to call the art director immediately for instructions.

This was weird; I never had to call an art director first.

On the phone he mentioned I'd have to fit into an outfit Christina wore in the movie for the poster and they were going to curl my hair. The shot involved Christina with long, wavy hair looking out of a window toward the city. It was going to be a back shot, so he said my hair length was going to be very important.

Didn't he know my hair was short? Shit.

I could hear him sigh over the phone in annoyance when I told him. He was upset since my agency told him my hair was longer and there was no time now to book another model.

Damn, it was my fault. I hadn't updated the agency with my shorter hair style.

Upsetting the art director and my agency weighed on my mind. Both my agency's reputation and mine were at stake.

I had to think of something quick since I wanted the job. I had to fix this situation. The job would look great on my resume. And the check for $400 would be good also. I told the art director, *"I'll make it work. See you tomorrow morning."*

Shit, I had to get to Union Square as soon as possible since all the stores were closing soon. I calculated the quickest subway route there from downtown and raced to the subway, the 4 train.

Once at Ricky's I felt like I was in a drag-queen's closet—wigs, boas, feathers, and the smell of hairspray and hair dye in the air. I clicked my heels over to the hair extensions and told the lady at the counter:

I need hair that's long and curly.

I was spastic over the prices. I hardly had enough money to get to Ricky's, but here I am pouring out $80 for fucking clip-in hair extensions. I didn't even know how to put these things in. But figuring I couldn't succeed unless I tried I bought the cheapest decent looking clip-on hair extensions I could find which I hoped wouldn't fry under the heat of a professional curling iron.

As I ran back to the Union Square station, dodging heavy raindrops, I called the hair salon that had just cut my hair a few days before. I was lucky someone answered the phone

2

before they closed. Breathing heavily into my cell phone, with my big pink Ricky's bag in hand, I begged the hair stylist to see me first thing the next morning. Thankfully she agreed.

Groggy, the next morning I sat in front of a huge mirror at the salon watching the stylist take the pieces of hair out of the bag and plop them on the table. I waited, hoping they would look OK, as one by one she clipped and pinned them tightly to my head. My scalp was starting to get sore, but I knew the tighter the better if I was going to pull this off. Then forty minutes later I stood up.

Wow, this just might work. I look like a goddess!

I thanked her with my last $20. Her facial expression appeared as if she took pity on me, taking my mediocre offer. I felt embarrassed, but to let her know I wasn't taking advantage of her I promised to tell everyone I knew about the salon on 13th Street and 6th Avenue, and raced to 22nd and Broadway.

I waltzed into the shoot – on time with coffee in hand – with confidence. My hair full of volume and lush. No one, not even the art director, second-guessed if the hair extensions would work or not. It was as if the conversation with him on the phone the night before was just a dream. Even the stylist they hired complimented me on the long locks as she teased them a few times before the shot.

Then I put on one of the outfits from the movie and went on set with my long locks and perfectly portrayed Christina Ricci's backside.

Sometimes to get the job done successfully you have to go the extra distance – this time it happened to be by hair length.

Subject: fit model booking for Teen Vogue
Don't wear any makeup. You will be trying on clothing and shoes.

My foot was being tortured and it was bleeding.

I was slow in placing my throbbing foot into the dainty, yet beautiful, 100-year-old-like shoe. In a weird way I felt like one of Cinderella's evil step sisters, trying to make my foot fit in the fragile glass slipper. Everyone was waiting for me to put it on. But it really was too small and I really was afraid I would break the shoe.

Because the shoe was so old and beaten there were small nails and shoe trimmings scraping the side of my foot. But the stylist couldn't care less. Red marks, that looked like cat scratches, were all over my feet. My pinky toe hurt, it matched my swollen big toe but I couldn't show it. I had to just suck it up and place my abused and bruised foot into the shoe each time we changed an outfit, adding stockings or a whole new look.

5

A part of me wanted to leave, screw it!
Yet a bigger part of me wanted this credit on my resume. And I wasn't one to give up half way through the race. I'm a fighter.

Each time the shoe scraped against the side of my foot, it made a deeper cut and bled a little more. I thought about the scars they might leave on my feet, preventing me from ever working a shoe modeling job again.

"These vintage shoes should be in a museum," I said sarcastically. Wishing they weren't on my feet.

Not knowing what else to say about the bloody mess pooling from the vintage torture devices on my feet, I just said:

"I'm sorry, can I have a tissue?" like some gamine beggar. The pair of stylists just rolled their eyes at me, like I was a weakling.

The only upside was that the clothing I got to wear were amazing. I especially liked the MaxMara dress, the Omo Norma Kamali leggings, the Moschino sequined cardigan, the Luella plaid dress, and the Jill Stuart metallic dress.

A few months later when the magazine came out, Rachel Bilson was glowing on the front cover and the outfits I had once worn did look amazing. Unfortunately for me the battered shoe I battled through never got its time to shine, it was left out of the editorial shots that made it into the magazine.

Even though there is never credit to the fit model in the magazine, getting the opportunity to put my pint-sized body to use is what energizes me. And a little blood can't defeat me.

New item to add to the model safety kit: Band-Aid.

Subject: confirm shoot for Marshalls
1/2 day Monday
8 a.m. call time
details to follow
you are going directly to central park

At the crack of dawn I raced up Wall Street and pranced toward the Trinity Church to the 4/5 train. I was still living out of a suitcase, but I had basically moved into my boyfriend's studio at 63 Wall Street.

On my way up Wall Street, I get the daily whistles and smiles from the security guys by The New York Stock Exchange, a policeman on a horse, some random tourists, and even the preacher man preaching about God gave me a glance. It was quite a walk up the slight hill to Broadway, and I always felt a little guilty telling people to *fuck off* so early in the morning, — but it didn't stop me from rolling my eyes and telling them to go to hell anyway, even one of God's chosen.

9

As usual, I do the worst thing you can possibly do on the subway – moisturize my legs. Slipping your toes out of your shoe and rubbing lotion on your feet and legs just screams to be gawked at by male transit riders. When I am finished, I attempted another dangerous trick and curled my eye lashes while in motion. The woman across from me stared in fright. I guess some of my actions call for being gawked at, but I have to rush to the job.

I had the motion of the train, the breaks, and the speed all in my mind as I clenched the eyelash curler. But practice makes perfect, and I loosened it just before the train jerked to a stop. My eyeballs and lashes were totally fine – perfectly curled actually. It is something I consider a skill.

Then, I looked in my journal and confirmed my destination:

8 a.m. Central Park at 72nd Street and 5th Avenue.

Got it.

I stood up a little too soon and waited by the subway doors looking at my reflection in the windows until the train pulled into the station. Right before I was about to bitch out the scruffy man behind me who was breathing down my back, the subway doors opened.

I raced through the station. I had to get to a hill near the Bethesda Fountain; I think it was Cherry Hill. I was supposed to be looking for a huge white trailer. You'd think it wouldn't be hard to find, but I was almost in a panic as it reached 8:15 a.m. and I had still not found the trailer. Being on time is a must for models and I pride myself for always being on time. I

10

was about to call my agency to confirm the location when I thankfully ran into one of the production assistants.

Inside the trailer clothing, shoes and hangers were sprawled everywhere. I settled into their craft service breakfast. Free food was usually tempting, but for now coffee was all I needed until the stylist was ready for me.

As I waited, I hid my feet until I had to show them. That's because a couple of days earlier I had stubbed my big toe on my boyfriend's fancy coffee table and under the toenail it looked like a purple sharpie marker dot. It might have been just a little dot to someone else, but for someone who uses her feet to book modeling jobs it was something worth hiding. I mixed some foundation into the bruise to cover it and hoped no one would notice it.

I was direct booked because I was a size-six shoe, so it wasn't like I wasn't going to do this job even with the bruise. And I wanted to keep my relationship with my agency as an always-available-model. And I wanted the money also, $1,000. Just for a shot of my freaking foot in a shoe--hell yeah! I'm very fond of this getting "direct booked" thing.

This would also be my first print shoe modeling job. I had moved up from shoe showrooms to print modeling campaigns. *Yes!* I did many seasons of shoe showroom modeling for *LifeStride, Naturalizer, Hot Kiss,* and many others. I was even flown to Vegas multiples times for shoe shows with all expenses paid, plus an additional $350 a day for the actual shoe modeling work.

11

Really getting the Marshalls booking came down to want and desire. I wanted to be more; I wanted print. So I created a comp card that showed my feet, and the photos on the card looked as if they could be ads. I sent these comp cards off to some of the top body parts agencies out there and now I was shooting for a real ad campaign. Being in print – even if it was just my foot – felt like being at a higher level in modeling.

My body is my asset as a model. A bruise could mean not getting hired or pissing someone off. And my goal was to make these Marshalls' people think, *"even if the model has a little bruise on her big toe, she's a great model, so we don't care."*

Finally, the stylist was ready for me and my feet. There were a couple selective outfits the stylist wanted me to now try on. I would be wearing a skirt. And for a moment I had thought *"Great, maybe more of me will be seen in the shot,"* since I was also given a top and a jacket. But today the *star* would be my leg, calves, ankles and toes.

It was a fall campaign, and I figured maybe it would be a bootie or a cute platform shoe that covered my toes and the bruise wouldn't matter. But then I saw the purple peep-toe pump in the stylist's hands and I knew I'd have to tell her about my issue.

The stylist didn't smile about it, but she suggested the makeup artist put another dab of foundation on the skin under my big toenail. She covered it up pretty well.

After a short walk to the first shooting location my personal sandals were replaced by the size-six patent leather peep-toe

12

pumps. I hoisted up with help from two gracious male photo assistants and sat on the railing of the lower podium with the *Angel of the Waters* fountain behind me. After angling my legs they debated the potential of the shot due to the shadows – the location would not do. The photographer moved us to the Bethesda Terrace stairs, which the art director agreed was a better place. And they set up once again.

Side note: Let me just be honest here. The money is damn good but sometimes being a shoe model involves facing some major discomfort. I fit a size six shoe but everyone knows putting a foot in a new shoe hurts! It's raw, stiff, and is going to continue to hurt until the shoe is broken in. This shoe was so cute but it was also super tight. It felt like I was standing on pins and needles. It was a blister in the making.

With fake leaves sprawled around the steps, I pretended to glide up the Bethesda Terrace stairs on the beautiful fall day. Of course my pose on the stairs meant the bruised toe was facing the camera. For a moment I worried, but then I focused on the task at hand of making the shoe look great. There wasn't anything to be worried about with a makeup artist nearby.

Most of the time I held my hands on my waist and focused on being as still as a mannequin, while making my foot look as alive as possible in each pose.

They took about 20 shots of each pose, click. Click. Click.

Soon, they have all the shots they need.

13

When the image appeared in the Marshalls fall campaign, it looked great! Never let a little imperfection prevent you from giving your best.

Subject: Stacy London show
full body nude
don't forget your robe

I felt elite stepping into a town car that afternoon. I always do when the client arranges a car, and I thought back to days when even paying for train fare was a burden. My call time today was later than usual, 3:30 p.m.

Although being in a car in mid-day traffic didn't make the trip to Midtown any quicker, as I was becoming very late. I let go of my privileged feeling and knew that taking the subway probably would have been faster.

The anxiety started to run up my back. Despite being two blocks away from my original destination on Seventh Avenue, I told the driver I had to get out in a frantic mess. Grabbing for my bag and my cell phone, I forced the door open in a hurry and was already half-way out before the driver yelled at me to sign his voucher. Outside on Seventh Avenue I quickly meshed into the street traffic. A few F.I.T. students with art portfolios and men with briefcases bumped into me, but I was in too much of a rush to care.

15

Soon, I saw my destination – New York's Hotel Pennsylvania, across from Madison Square Garden and Penn Station, in the Grand Ballroom.

The Grand Ballroom is where popular television shows have been filmed, previously *The Maury Povich Show* and *Sally Jessy Raphael* and *The People's Court* were filmed there.

My role for today: I would appear completely nude in front of a live audience for the *Fashionably Late with Stacy London* talk show. It was a segment offering tips on looking good naked. At least it was a compliment; since I was an example of "looking good."

I was directed to the elevator and on my way up I thought about a recent casting for a skincare brand when I had to take off my top and show my shoulders and backside. Today baring it all for a live audience wasn't a big deal. Another day. Another job. With or without clothing or a garment rack. I considered being comfortable with my body an asset.

As I entered the complex I was met by a production assistant. Together we zigzagged through a quartet of dancers, up some stairs, hopscotched over huge electrical cords, past a hallway of random background extras, and landed in a waiting room with two big couches, a plasma TV, and a table of food.

Perfect. I plopped my bag down and sat cozily. As I rubbed cream on my legs, and glad to be in a quiet place to prepare for my disrobing, I was welcomed by three other girls.

The threesome were here to be *"told off"* for their lack of fashion sense by the famous style expert TV host, Stacy

16

London, and then be given brand new outfits on the segment – sort of like a fashion makeover. It sounded cute. I actually almost felt like the "weirdo" of the bunch without an outfit to burn. But mostly these girls were excited to get a goodie bag at the end of the filming.

They asked what I would be doing here.

"I'm here to be naked," I mentioned casually.

One laughed and covered her mouth. *"I could never do that!"* she exclaimed.

I explained that as a model I did a lot of "body jobs" where I show off my figure – my feet, my hands, my legs, my butt, my chest – to display products like creams or whatever. I rambled off a grocery list of work I'd done. Even so, they couldn't believe I was comfortable unclothed in front of strangers. I just smiled.

As the small talk ended I refocused on my body. I tried to remember, *did I shave everything?* I checked my crotch discreetly with my hand when the girls weren't looking, wondering: *Is the camera going to zoom in on me?*

My agent had said *"you will walk onstage naked -- that's it. Should take a couple of minutes, they will probably blur things during the broadcast."*

But still, I wasn't sure how much of my nude body would be seen. I had an American Apparel tube top dress on and I scooted it up a little and ran my hands up and down my legs. I could feel a little stubble I missed by my ankle, and went to

17

reach for my emergency bag full of "model touch ups": shavers, tweezers, and clear nail polish.

But before I could, I heard someone peek into the room and ask, *"Is the nude model here?"*

That was my cue to get my hair and makeup done. The other girls stared in disbelief. They looked at me as if I was preparing to walk the plank.

On the way to hair chair, one of the production assistant's asked politely; *"Are you over 18? Are you OK being fully nude?"* I guess they weren't sure if I was legal since I look younger than I am and I calmed their nerves by laughing it off saying I was totally fine. *"And yes, I'm in my twenties."*

While getting my makeup done, I chatted with the editor of a women's magazine who was going to be in the segment with me. She mentioned she often used body part models for her magazine. I made a mental note to leave her my modeling comp card before I left.

When my hair and makeup was done, the production assistant chirped, *"It's time!"* I peeled off my tube dress completely, threw it in my bag, quickly slipped on a robe and left wearing only that and my sexy black high heels.

As I walked to the set I reached down and touched my crotch and my breast a few more times through my robe to make sure I was all ready. The production assistant would take my robe when the segment began. She would also be there to meet me on the other side of the set after the segment was over to slip the robe back on me. That was the plan.

As I peeked from behind the curtain I felt some chills run up my spine. It was a full audience! They were waiting, like I was, for the segment to begin. I studied the set, took notice of where the camera was and then practiced my strut a few times. I felt my ego run up my legs. I could do it.

As the moment drew closer I took off my robe confidently and handed it to the production assistant. As I waited I felt the cold air say *hello*. I focused on the black tape on the ground – my mark – and I looked up as Stacy entered the set. She excited the crowd with her savvy and sassy fashionista voice.

Offstage watching her for the first several minutes of the show, I played with my hair and almost forgot I was naked. Then I heard the host yell, *"Come on out, Isobella!"*

As I took my first steps from behind the curtain, I could see Stacy was eyeing me from head to toe. She pointed at me and asked the magazine editor, *"So, how do I get a body like that?"*

I could feel the camera out of the corner of my eye zooming in on me, the lights embracing my bare skin. I walked to my mark and took a model pose, with one knee bent to show attitude and with my chin up. I glued my hands on my hips and I let out a huge poised smile. I even made eye contact with a few audience members, then I looked to left and winked at Stacey.

The lights on the set were warming me up, and my body loved the attention. With dignity I arched my back and turned my body with a little shake, showing my backside. I felt like I was moving too fast so then I slowed my movements down and casually looked down at my body for a second, admiring it. I let my hands grace my stomach and moved my shoulders in a sexy, sensual sway. I felt tall, like the Giraffes at Ford Models.

I imagined myself as a naked Miss America.

I was on set much longer than I thought I would be. It was exhilarating to get more air time – letting my body glow in the studio lights and having my moment.

Stacy joked that I should get going since I might get a cold standing around naked. I winked at her one more time and started my catwalk, crossing the set and the audience clapping. I ducked through the curtains and as promised, the production assistant greeted me with a robe.

The production folks congratulated me like I had won the Olympics. One even gave me a hug.

Back in the waiting room, I put the rest of my clothes on. And when the magazine editor arrived I gave her my comp card. Soon after that, the other girls returned and received the goodie bags. I wanted a goodie bag as well, but quickly decided it was fine. Being paid to do what I love, even if it involves full nudity, beats a goodie bag any day!

20

Subject: Confirm Saturday *Time* magazine
it's a breast cancer story -- so topless
very well respected photographer
it will be in the afternoon

The lights were warm but my nipples were hard. As a chill ran up my spine goosebumps formed on my arm and my tummy tightened. The task today was to be topless for a story based on breast cancer around the world. The world map would be projected on my bare chest in a few minutes, but right now I was just taking a quick test shot to see if the lights were positioned correctly.

When it was time to shoot I would gently push together my breasts with the sides of my upper arms; to get a little more cleavage.

The photographer fit the rustic personality of the antique Carnegie Hall Artist Studio he worked in, and his thin-rimmed glasses and blond boy hair gave him this artistic wizard appeal. The studio was covered with little trinkets and sculptures here and there; I was scared to touch the secret wonders which were probably at least 100 years old and that

21

sat collecting dust. It seemed like they inspired his work each day.

The magazine editor was also there, observing everything and spending her Saturday off really working with us. With a neatly buttoned blouse, and glasses she took on and off, she gushed sweetly over the photographer's work and the joy of working with him again.

I had taken off my tank top and the makeup artist was now airbrushing a light coat of foundation on my arms, shoulders, collarbone, neck, breasts, belly button, and stomach. I would reappear on the set when it had dried.

Everyone there knew I would be topless during shooting so there was nothing to hide. But instead of showing my nipples boldly at the start, I just cupped my chest in my hands politely until I got on set and waited to be instructed that the photographer was ready. But the photographer couldn't be ready until the assistant had everything in place.

It seemed to take a long time to set everything up. Patiently, yet growing more impatient as time passed, I was starting to get cold but kept my mouth shut about it.

"Ok we're all set," the assistant finally announced and I walked over to my mark on the set. Standing in front of the tripod and still cupping myself, I waited for some direction. But the photographer liked how I was just standing there – with my head slightly turning down – and told me *"just stay how you are."*

22

He went towards the camera, looking forward to the shot, telling me over and over not to move. He put his eye to the viewfinder and pressed down on the shutter button.

Nothing happened.

I waited for the click but didn't hear it. No beautiful click!

The lack of the sound of the shutter accomplishing the shot startled everyone.

I stayed in my pose – head down, cupping my chest – then looked up with my eyes to see if anything was wrong.

Something was.

The photographer just huffed. He couldn't believe it. The assistant didn't have the camera ready and we missed a beautiful shot. The room was silent and I continued to wait until the assistant could figure out what the heck was wrong and fix it as soon as possible. I felt bad for the apologetic assistant, bad for the photographer who just missed the shot he wanted, and the magazine photo editor wondering what was going on. They all watched me as they waited for the right cord to be plugged in so that the shot could be taken properly.

The assistant was obviously embarrassed. I hate it when people are embarrassed. I always feel the urge to ease the situation, but for now, doing my best to hold my pose was all I could do to help the situation.

Because the photographer was trying to get over his frustration, the first shots went terribly of course. With the camera now functioning, the assistant became busy adjusting and playing with the projector. Getting the globe perfect across my torso was his next task. The whole process reminded me of my 8th grade teacher fumbling with a projector he had no idea how to use.

The assistant would eventually make it look good. He had to; the photographer didn't want to Photoshop it in. He wanted to capture the projection that appeared on my chest as it was.

Finally, after the first quality images were observed, the editor of the magazine commented that *"this might be the cover shot!"*

All of our ears woke up to the sound of that!

The shot would start at my chin and go down to my belly button. I would tilt my head to show a profile and nuzzle my chin into the top of my shoulder.

My body acted like a screen. Africa appeared in the middle of my chest. Then the photographer moved the laminated sheet a little and soon it was covering one of my breasts. Russia and China appeared to, on my other breast. The continents came out a purple and red color.

He took a few shots with some different variations, some with my arms and hands hugging my body and some with my hands on my hips. Then Brazil was on my belly button and he went around the world deciding what continents he would shoot next. The magazine editor chimed in with a few suggestions. I had every country on my torso that afternoon, even down my arms and on my sides.

24

It was quite a creative day! The shots were truly amazing. Unfortunately the tear-sheet and cover never made it in my portfolio. The magazine later decided to use a totally different image and model. Oh well, it's all part of a day in the life of being a model. After the day is done, you never know what

will happen to the images; if they will be edited, used or not used after all.

Subject: interested in doing a nude?
airbrush, lingerie shoot

There's an arrangement of feathers, sequins, rhinestones, lace and silk, scattered on a table nearby. It's ready to be applied to my body.

A pair of lace panties and thigh high stockings will soon be airbrushed onto the backside of my body. Then a rhinestone heart tattoo will be placed where my spine grooves and starts to arch above my behind.

When it's showtime, the stylist pulls at my robe gently, tells me to stand in front of her and says casually, *"lift your robe hunny."* So I reveal my shaven *"chick-lit."*

She admires it for a moment, like a medical student. Then praises how I shaved and pans her next move.

Her forefinger and thumb stretch and measure the width between my bikini lines. While measuring, she hums a Polish song; she has a soft voice and it's soothing. She carefully cuts

27

a piece of silk cloth into a square and adds three dabs of some "special body glue" to my skin. Then puts the silk square against my *"chick-lit."* I feel the warmth of her hand pressing the fabric against me softly. It sticks and stays. I now have a silk loincloth, and the openness of the air suddenly makes my *"chick-lit"* feel loose and free down there. For the next nine hours the tiny square fabric will act as an itty bitty curtain down there.

My bare back and my lower body will be the focus for the shot, so the small loincloth covering in front is really for my own privacy. A part of me feels like I'm a scandalous Pocahontas.

While the stylist decides which piece of lace will soon be pressed against my skin and stenciled to my body; I do some B-roll video sharing the concept of the day's shoot.

Finally, it's time to airbrush on some thigh high fishnets. Yay!

I stand on two wooden apple boxes. For once, I am the tallest one in the room! My butt is at eye level when the stylist sits on her work chair.

First, a base is applied. A golden powdered pigment patted up and down the back of my legs, and fully rubbed in to cover my whole leg – butt, thigh, toes and all.

I feel like the Emmy Awards golden goddess statuette!

There is a technique to airbrushing thigh high fishnet stockings on the body, it's an artistic skill.

First, I actually have to put on a real pair of fishnets stockings. She slowly slides them up my leg; she does all the work to ensure the golden pigment stays on my leg. It's actually intriguing, and erotic, to have someone else put fishnets on you!

She is about to start airbrushing black paint against the open spaces of the fishnet stockings. I must stay as still as possible during this part, even though it's cold and tingly against my skin.

After around thirty minutes, she peels the real pair of fishnet stockings off. The stencil that remains is so perfect that from only a few feet away it looks as if I still had the real fishnet thigh highs on my legs.

But she has only begun!

A piece of white lace is now put against my thigh and airbrushed over to look like a gorgeous stenciled lace trimming above the fishnet.

Then, ribbons of burgundy sequins are glued across the back of my thigh to make the rim of where the lace meets the fishnet even more seductive. I can't help but start to feel sexier with each step.

Each time she touches my skin and adds detail with her thin paintbrush, I am reminded of my nudity. Thank God for the loincloth and that four-inch bit of privacy. But I keep my knees straight and still when she says, *"Don't move hunny."*

I am there to do a job. But still hanging out behind the loincloth for hours is bringing many sensations down there. How awkward. It's not that I was sexually turned on by the experience, or her, but guess the lower body has a mind of its own sometimes.

Now it's time to airbrush the lace panty on my behind. To do this, an actual piece of lace is placed across my butt. Then to make the panties look as realistic as possible, the stylist has to airbrush and hold the lace in place at the same time to create the perfect low rise panties. The difficult part is keeping the lace in place between my butt cheeks. There's not a tool proper enough to hold the lace in place between there! So the stylist grabs her thin paintbrush and secures it between my cheeks. We all laugh, but it will just have to do.

Next, twenty-five red and orange rhinestones are pressed on my ass. With the paint, sequins, rhinestones and airbrushed fishnets, I started to feel like a *Sports Illustrated Swimsuit Issue* model during her airbrush bikini experience.

Five hours into the process, lunch finally comes and is served. As I scoop out some lasagna and suck the butter out of a bread roll, the photographer politely yet firmly says *"Just, whatever you do, don't sit down!"*

Even when I had to go to the bathroom throughout the day, I had to be extremely careful when I squat over the toilet, so not to ruin the airbrush design.

We are finally ready to shoot. Facing the black silk backdrop with my ass to the camera, I am told the inspiration is to give poses like a German model that is pissed and with a fuck you attitude.

Two male assistants hide behind the black silk backdrop and shake it furiously while a fan blows from behind the backdrop. The result is very lush, wavy silk, and I playfully reach for it. I am standing, but was given direction to reach upwards to simulate the look of lying on a silk bed and enjoying the feel of the fabric. And I did, it felt real good.

For how long the preparation work took, it seemed like the actual shooting went so fast. Though after nine full hours of standing, we wrap up. I was sad when it was all over.

My body ached! It was a lot of stretching, arching, bending, waiting...never being able to sit down throughout the whole process. But the most painful thing was the trip home. Even though I was wearing my comfortable Raggedy-Anne busted sweatpants on the E train heading downtown, the rhinestones pinched my ass as I sat. It felt like little I was sitting on hundreds of individual pebbles.

It took a few days for the airbrush paint to completely come off my legs and butt, and my whole body was tender for the next couple of days. The soreness was a reminder of the type of creative energy that gets put into many shoots, and the endurance required to be a professional model.

As for the loincloth, like a Polaroid, I saved it as a memento.

Subject: Victoria's Secret Legs/Catalog
1/2 day starting at 10:30 a.m.

An assistant yelled to the photographer, *"The leg model is here!"*

The pressure was on.

The night before this go-see, I'd carefully prepared my legs. I shaved, covered the scar on my knee with some foundation, and lotioned them up about twelve times that night. Then applied one last smear of lotion on the train ride to the go-see.

I was nervous because this go-see would determine whether I nailed my first job as a leg model. I'd done other types of modeling before, but this was something new. Any time I try something I've never done, I feel a mix of nervousness and excitement, as well as determination to succeed.

"Ok, take off your shoes and put these sandals on," said the art director.

I was confused. When I read *leg casting* I hadn't considered my feet being judged today either. I typically am prepared, but this one caught me off guard, and my toes weren't perfectly pedicured.

Side note: Let this be a lesson to all models. When you go to a casting for one thing you should always be prepared for other things as well.

I started to take my stilettos off slowly while eyeing the fresh pair of sandals sitting on the table that I would soon be trying on. Just as I'd feared, my feet weren't looking as good as they could look. The art director, photographer and a handful of assistants stared at me and my feet. I felt like an idiot.

The shoot was for a sandal, a "fitness sandal" meant to tone your legs while you walk.

Then one of the assistants tapped the nearby table with her hands. It was a sign to climb on top of it. And I did.

I slipped on the fitness sandal and positioned my legs to show it off, while pointing my toes a little. The photographer and art director bent their bodies down towards my shins. They analyzed my legs and looked at the way the sandal fit my foot.

I turned slowly so they could see every angle of my legs and lifted up my skirt a little. Making my legs appear longer with one leg bent in front of the other.

I thought to myself, "*I hope they think my legs looked long enough,*" as I jump off the table.

34

As I put my stilettos back on, one of the evaluating ladies said, *"How do you walk in those things?"* I told her it was really easy, thinking to myself once again, *"I hope I get this job."* But I started to hate my shoes; they made my feet look like shit. I promised myself never to wear high heels to go-sees or castings again.

I left the go-see feeling terrible.

However, a few hours later I was bursting with excitement when my agent emailed me to say I booked the job. I would get $250 an hour for modeling my legs and feet for this shoe product. And there would be a makeup artist on set to prepare my legs before the shoot. The pictures would be featured in their catalog and on their website.

I pictured my legs being seen in the catalog! *"Take that tall giraffes!"*

****

The day of the shoot I showed up with a pedicure. A pretty French one – very neat and preppy. I was eager to show it off when I arrived.

Two production assistants rubbed my legs with this "special lotion" that they claimed would grease them but not streak. Then I put on a pair of cotton shorts and a tank top.

When they said, *"she's ready!"* I walked towards the set gleefully in the fitness sandals, red shorts, and a white tank top tied tight and pulled up so that my stomach showed.

I climbed a ladder and stood atop a platform three feet off the floor. This would be my stomping ground. A thick wood board was covered with a metallic reflecting sheet with a low barricade, creating a fake "pool" of water a few inches deep. One of the photographer's assistants stood at the far end of this mini-pool, spraying water to create the mood of movement.

I stepped into the pool of water. Then the photographer told me to *"make a splash!* It had to look natural and create enough water beads on my legs so that it looked like a person was really jumping in the puddle and was having fun in the water – not too hard but not too light either. There was a bar, like a ballet barre, that I could hold on to as I stomped in the pool.

Everyone watched as I practiced my stomp in the water. The water splashed and a stream ran down my leg. It was fun, like being told to do the things your mother always said not to do. I even splashed the photographer's assistant a couple times. It was amusing being allowed to get everyone wet.

But the practice was over soon enough and it was time to shoot the real thing, which consisted of a little multitasking. It involved a trick of holding the bar with one hand, tightening my tummy, not letting the other hand get in the shot, keeping the same stomp spot in my mind, staying in the frame, and stomping at the exact tenth of a second that the camera would click.

STOMP...STOMP.

Luckily we shot digital and they could quickly adjust which

36

way to move…a little to the left…a little to the right. I followed his hand motions which seemed to say, *"Back up a few inches. Ok. Try again."*

STOMP…STOMP.

There was always something to adjust. My left leg was too high; there was too much water on my right leg; the sandal was slipping off my foot. I thought I saw him stare at my scar on the side of my left knee, which was facing the camera. But then again, maybe not.

He mumbled something like, *"perhaps if we counted together we would get it just right?"*

1…2…3…STOMP!
Click!

"Again."

1…2…3…STOMP!
Click!

"Again."

I felt a little like a horse, preparing my stride. More STOMPING. I was soon in a rhythm.

1…2…3…STOMP!
Click!

"Again."

37

1...2...3...STOMP!
Click!

"Again."

The water got too wild again, spilling out the sides of the pool. The set was adjusted, water drained and refilled.

By the end of it, I was soaked from thigh to toe. I glanced over and saw the art director smile at the photos on the computer screen.

"I did it," I thought to myself. My legs looked great and that's what mattered. Everyone was smiling. Even the photographer gave me a few nods of acknowledgement.

When I received a photo at the end of the shoot, I had a new kind of confidence. Even the short model can use her legs to get the job done. Even for Victoria's Secret!

Subject: *Luna* magazine-Shoot Monday
shoot and the interview on Monday at 11 a.m. at the showroom of TOCCA

I had been getting some buzz about how I wrote my first book *Almost 5'4"* at the Apple Store when I was broke. In other words, when I was homeless and without my own computer. So the store had become my writing hub, a place to relax and collect my thoughts. It was my office, it was free.

I had used the store and their display computers for almost two years as my daily spot to check my emails, scout out modeling jobs and update my social media. It felt only natural to write my book there; it was convenient. I stood in front of an iMac for hours a day, and after about five months I had the manuscript. I then self-published my modeling memoir *Almost 5'4"*, and after that HarperCollins released it in the UK.

But after writing my manuscript at the store, I promoted my story and book by myself. MediaBistro.com's Fishbowl NY and Galleycat all published blogs featuring my story, and a stream of other news features soon followed.

Then an Italian reporter who was a regular contributor to the Italian magazine *LUNA* wrote me because her editor in Milan was interested in interviewing me and a planning a photo shoot for the magazine. When I saw the words *ITALIAN, MAGAZINE* and *MILAN* in the email my eyes OPENED. The reporter scheduled an appointment for me to visit a designer showroom in the city to prepare for the styling part of the photo shoot:

Hi Isobella.
We would like to do the shoot and the interview on Monday (Aug 11th) at 11 am at the showroom of TOCCA, in a beautiful loft at 542 west 22nd street.
Ciao

We confirmed my Tocca meeting. It was a thrill to have people making plans for a story around me. But it was even more exciting to have a fashion magazine wanting to shoot a short model.

The reporter said *"it would be great to have something Apple-ish for the story,"* and asked if I had a contact there or if it would be possible to shoot inside the store. I knew it would be tough. Just because you write a book at the Apple Store, are invited to do an Apple Store reading, and get some great media coverage on the experience from your own self promotion, doesn't mean the store will host your photo shoots. I expressed the difficulty that I foresaw in this and suggested that perhaps we could get a shot more discreetly and not so obvious.

"Maybe we could get some shots of me inside the store on an iMac near the front store window?" I said. I would walk into the store myself and casually go over to the computer by the window and play with it. The photographer would stay outside and get the shot of me through the window. Maybe we could be a bit sneaky and have him come inside and take the shot, but then again the last thing I wanted was to be kicked out or get in trouble with the store that allowed me to write my memoir and has always been so good to me. She agreed. I was sure the photographer could work his magic by staying on the outside.

Soon, I was taking the train uptown and meeting with the head of public relations lady of Tocca to try on outfits. Of course being a Google whore and diligent researcher, I studied the company beforehand and got excited over their femininity and detailed embroidery on their sensible and sweetly alluring collection. At the time, I could only dream of affording them.

~

The elevator door opened. I was in the middle of the Tocca studio living room and noticed the white hardwood floor and a cluster of beautiful crystal wall sconces. A vintage sofa and a huge unframed canvas hung purposely, carelessly, on the wall and a sweet golden dresser against the wall caught my eye.

A blonde, Swedish woman, who was probably also a model, was at the sweet little reception vanity table and welcomed me (She would later help me translate an upcoming feature I shot for the Swedish *Bon Magazine)*.

41

The blond Swedish woman then called for Tocca's head of public relations, who greeted me with two kisses, one on each cheek. She whisked me through their other showroom, a room full of perfumes and fragrances, candles, and laundry specialties.

During my tour I learned that Tocca was Italian for "touch." Not knowing this before I had entered Tocca definitely made me feel more like an Italian American and not a true Italian. It was embarrassing to tell the Italian associates that worked there how even though my family was from Naples and Messina, Sicily, I didn't speak Italian, and, at the time, also hadn't even been to Italy yet.

Like an Italian outcast I followed the Italian born PR lady; it felt like I was following Sophia Loren around. She had a sharp wit to her. So in my mind I gave her the nickname Sophia.

We met up with the PR assistant, who also doubled as a stylist, and we all went into the back room where I saw a huge closet. My eyes widened. I couldn't wait to try the clothing on. My hand slowly grazed over the racks of fabric like my fingers were stroking over the keys of a piano. It was like music to my ears.

Sophia and the PR assistant already prepared some of their favorite picks, and I was excited to slip on my first dress. They spoke very fast, and with passion. They switched constantly from English and Italian when talking to each other. Sometimes I only caught half of the conversation, but I could tell they had excitement in their voices about the garments they chose for the shoot. I felt special!

42

I did a spin in the dress. It was pinned a little since it was so small. The dress was "oooh'ed" over and then a digital picture was taken. I tried on about ten other outfits, including a beautiful long gray double-breasted tweed coat with an Oliver Twist feel to it. And everyone got hyper, it looked sleek. It would be perfect for the theme of the article based on my basically-homeless-living-at-the-Apple-store-every-day-writing-appeal since it was chic but still had the gamine feel to it.

I loved the Oliver Twist musical! I liked the sweetness, coy expressions, and sincerity Oliver had. How even in rags he was a cutie pie. I wanted him to sing to me *I'd do anything* (even though he only lip-synched it in the movie).

When I was done with the fitting I collected my bag and was preparing to leave. I overheard Sophia speaking Italian to some other assistants. Then she touched the ends of my hair and in English she said with a smile, *"Would you mind changing your hair color? It looks a little orange. Let's make it more Italian!"*

The way she said *Italian* made it sound like a really good idea. So I sang to her *"I'll do anything for you"* since I also thought it was a great idea. Sophia said come back here tomorrow afternoon and we'll dye your hair. We have a big bathroom here and it will be easy to do. Then I was handed a huge brown bag that had some clothing and samples inside —a present!

I left unsure if the people at Tocca liked me. I figured my hair must have looked pretty scraggly if they wanted to change it. I regretted going to the mediocre salon a few weeks before to get blond highlights. What a stupid idea that was. My hair turned out more orange than blond. Oh jeez, I even shot a feature with *The New York Post* with that hair too! I rolled my eyes at that one and rode the train back downtown, dwelling on my hair the whole time.

Later the *LUNA* reporter emailed me and said:

I heard the girls at Tocca loooved you!!!
You are going to look beautiful.
I will be there on Monday for the interview
can't wait,
Ciao

I was glad Sophia and the girls at Tocca liked me. Tomorrow, my hair would become a deep dark rich brown.

~

I remember my head was under the faucet for a very long time, and closed my eyes as the water trickled down the sides of my face. Sophia and her watchful assistants waited patiently as my hair became more Italian. I don't remember what the hair dye bottle looked like, but it wasn't a familiar brand. It probably was imported from Italy. *Real* Italian rich brown. She told me it brought back my Italian blood.

This time, I left with a bag of Tocca candles.

I had been so broke and overcoming living out of a suitcase at the time. So these were major luxuries to me and I would only light them a few times to preserve them.

When I got home from the showroom there was already an email from Sophia, who *asked "Do you like your new Italian hair color?"*

She was so sweet; she was concerned if I was mad about it.

Maybe my smile wasn't big enough after the hair dying, but I wasn't mad at all. I was in fact happy. My hair was a beautiful dark sultry color and I loved it. After the shoot I would not go back to my weird orange tinted hair, and never went back to that salon either. I would let my natural brown grow back after the dark dye faded.

~

The day of the shoot I first wore a fluffy ruffled white buttoned blouse under the Oliver Twist coat, dark gray capri pants, and a pair of very high maroon stilettos. I felt like a giraffe even though everyone around was still taller than me. The coat was heavy, but the weight of it on my shoulders made me feel powerful. The gorgeous Buccellati jewelry around my neck made me feel even more powerful, as a security guard in the corner of the room kept his watchful eye on the jewels throughout the day.

They all watched as I carelessly sat in a vintage chair, with my legs hung over one of the arms and the cape of the long coat flowing to the floor. There were the two beautiful crystal wall sconces, the painting and the gold dresser in the background. I gave a take-no-shit-attitude stare at the camera; I felt like a refined female version of Oliver Twist.

45

Afterward, the *LUNA* reporter asked me questions about my journey as a short model, the Apple Store, and life. Then we were off to SoHo, since the group really wanted an Apple Store shot. One of these images would become the opening shot for the article.

It was around 1 p.m. when we arrived in SoHo, a very busy time of day for the area. Usually by 10 a.m. the streets are already packed. It was a hot August day and I was wearing a warm cream colored faux fur coat that went to my waist, with the cute little hood on my head.

For this shot I stood in front of the huge glass doors of the Apple Store, with the long iconic glass staircase in the background. I hugged myself slightly, with one hand reaching my shoulder and the other wrapped around my side. The shot had a mysterious feeling to it. I was looking in the distance, as if I was waiting on time to arrive, and figuring out my next move.

Then I ran into the Apple Store with the next outfit in my hands and changed in the bathroom as fast as I could. It was a perfect set up. Actually, the Apple Store bathroom has always been useful to me over the years. I've changed there many times before castings and to touch up my face. And the facilities are usually clean.

When I went down the glass stairs I walked directly over to a computer by the window, like we had planned, and the photographer clicked away from the outside.

That afternoon we took over SoHo. We went through so many wardrobes that it felt like I wore the whole Tocca fall

46

collection. They were beautiful and exquisite. And although I already knew how it felt to accomplish a modeling job for a brand, product or magazine, this time it felt different. This shoot was based around me striving to do what I love. It was the feature on me – probably the tiniest model to be in an Italian fashion magazine.

By giving yourself a chance and not being afraid to self promote, you might see yourself in an Italian magazine as well.

Subject: Avail this afternoon? *Woman's World* pedicure story
you need to go there right now!

I am the "Last Minute Model." As soon as you say when, I'm on my way. But sometimes being available isn't enough. Like the time when I was available for a weekend shoot as a stand in for Tina Fey for *Vanity Fair* magazine. They wanted a 34B. I wear a 32B.

Other times, being available was all I needed to land the job. One of these last minute jobs happened to be with *Woman's World* magazine for a summer pedicure editorial based on do-it-yourself pedicures and how easy they were to do. The shoot was at 873 Broadway between 18th and 19th (it was actually the same building where I body doubled for Christina Ricci, but I was going to a different studio this time).

My agency said the editor wasn't happy with the first models that were sent, so now a "backup" was being sent—me! I was told they had a nail stylist on set and that I didn't need to get my pedicure done a certain color. Just show up! So I quickly hopped on the W train, and when I got to Union Square I flew up Broadway.

When I got there a couple editorial assistants greeted me enthusiastically. Then I took off my shoes to show them my feet to examine. I had my portfolio ready for inspection as well. They examined each toe, approved me, and probably emailed my agency. I was booked for the rest of the day

I settled in and notice there were a couple other models here. I recognized one from other castings. She was getting a pedicure from the nail stylist, while another girl was waiting her turn. It wasn't small talk time, the whole studio was keeping busy and the nail stylist looked really tired already. I wondered how many shots they had done that morning and how many were left to do.

Soon another girl came in. Her toes were reviewed and approved as well. But time was slipping away and it was almost noon. She soon became my buddy. But instead of working with the nail stylist we were sent to the closest nail salon we could find, a tactic by the assistant editor to save time and get a first coat of color for our toenails and fingernails. We were each handed a nail polish color and off we went. Mine was a hot pink polish. My buddy had a light pink. She was also handed some cash from the editor so we could pay for the salon visit.

At the salon up the street, there was a wait, at least 15 minutes. We debated going to another salon, but we figure that by the time we found another salon it would hopefully be our turn. We got antsy; the assistant had said to be as fast as we could. So when we finally got into the pedicure chair we told the nail technicians we needed the fastest pedicure and manicure in the world. It felt like an hour has passed and I started to worry about time. I usually enjoy pedicures, but I was so anxious to get back to the shoot that this one caused a panic attack. I told the nail technician to just do a little lotion, I didn't need the full thing, and to skip the pumice stone scrub (I usually skip the pumice stone scrub anyways since I think about the thousands of women's feet who have been scrubbed with it and worry about germs).

Then, my buddy and I carefully pranced over to the manicure tables. Even more time has passed now and my anxiety increased as each nail gets painted. We knew there was not time to sit and wait for our fingernails to fully dry, so as soon as the last stroke hit our last fingernail we jumped up and quickly paid – making sure to take our nail polishes with us as well.

Side note: I often bring my own nail polish to salons. It is best to own it and therefore comes in handy for any touch ups you might need if you get a chip or something.

Back at the photo studio, dazzle was then added to the toes. I waited while another model got a plaid yellow and orange looking design added to her big toe. Then I had to wait longer since my buddy was going to get her dazzle done before me. She was getting a pretty pink French pedicure. I had a thirty minute wait so I decided to use the Internet on my cell phone. But it was so slow it was pitiful; I chose the alternative of writing in my journal and made a to-do list for the next day.

Finally, my name was called. Because this was a step-by-step editorial, we had to shoot all the steps.

51

I took my sandals off before I went on set, then I placed my feet on the yellow blanket. The shot for the editorial involved acting like I was doing my own toe-nails, step by step painting them and the editorial would explain how to create the design.

This shot was basic, since it was just of the hot pink base color on the toes. I took the nail polish brush out of the bottle and held the brush near my big toe.

The brush had a dab of hot pink nail polish on it and I thought myself, "I hope I don't spill any on the yellow blanket." And of course I did.

Shit! This made the photo assistant freak out. She quickly folded the yellow blanket and adjusted it. I already made her do extra work and we just starting shooting. But we got the shot they needed. Then I skedaddled off set and waited for the nail stylist to add the next step to my toes.

Next, I listened to editor of the magazine who had the presence of a respectable Queen tell the nail stylist what she should do to my nails next.

So the nail stylist started a pretty flower design on one of my big toes. But then I noticed that she was making a mistake. The plan was to create two flowers on my big toe using neon yellow nail polish. And each flower should have four dotted pedals and one dot in the center.

Oh no! I noticed the stylist put five pedals on one flower and sure enough, when my toes were inspected by the Queen, that toe had to be redone and repainted.

So off went everything, the neon yellow and hot pink polish and all. Oh jeez!

It was nerve-racking to sit there and watch the nail stylist mess up again. Strike two. And again, strike three. I felt sorry for her because I sure of hell probably couldn't complete this do-it-yourself nail design myself.

The two flowers and the dots had to be so perfectly placed to create the pedals. Perfectly! Finally, it looks like she gets it right this time and I go to the Queen again for inspection. Yes! The toes are approved. Now it's time to shoot this shit.

Side note: My big toes have a large nail bed and this was the day my big toes could shine. It was perfect for the flower designs!

Once again I had to pretend to paint my nail and add the yellow dots this time. It was frightening to have to be very still and not ruin the flower design which had already been redone over and over again. I feared I'd fuck it up, but my fear made my hand even steadier and I got through it.

Then I had to put on hot pink shoes with rhinestones on them. They were a couple sizes too big, but we could cheat that since the shot was from the front of my foot.

Lying on my back with my legs up on a stool, pushing my toes forward to reach the rim of the shoes, and then making my feet look relaxed and pretty was not easy. It was very uncomfortable.

My mind was working so hard to control my feet, point my toes, and make them look pretty that I accidently kicked over the vase of pink and yellow flowers on the stool. The vase hit the floor with a huge bang and water spilled everywhere. Oh God!

This obviously wasn't a highlight of the day, but I held onto my confidence and was eager to accomplish the shot.

Later, when the editorial came out in print my toes would be the first thing you saw, —you'd never assume there were any redo's, or that the vase of flowers spilled all over the set, or drops of hot pink nail polish got on the yellow blanket numerous times.

Sometimes things don't always go perfect on the job, but you keep working for the best result. Having patience for myself and forging past the moments of anxiety and mistakes showed me once again that being a model takes an attitude of perseverance.

Subject: casting Monday for Macy's
they would like to see you at 10:30 a.m. Steiner studios
this is for hands – TV commercial
they need someone petite for this

I had to get to Brooklyn. It sounded like a hell of a hike, but because it was I was actually more inclined to attend. I figured fewer models would show up, making my chances to book the job higher. Going to Brooklyn is like going to another world, and Steiner Studios which is way over at the Brooklyn Navy Yard, was a pain in the ass to get to.

I decided to skip the subway and then try to figure out the Brooklyn bus system, it would have pissed me off if I got lost. So I jumped in a cab. Spending money to get to a casting is a pain, but I want to get this job since I need money, and sometimes you have to spend money to make money.

I gazed at the skyline of Manhattan out of the cab window as we went over the Brooklyn Bridge. I moisturized my hands and arms, and touched up my mascara en route.

55

The cab drove up to the studio's security blockade and I yelled through the window to the security guy, *"Hi, I am here for a Macy's casting."* I thought he would just let us in, but he wouldn't. He had to check his list and make sure I was on it. I told him my name and it wasn't on the list. Shit! The cab's meter was still running. So I told the cab driver I would get out, not knowing yet if I could even get into the casting.

I kept saying *"Macy's, it's a casting,"* but also wondered if no one had showed up for this one besides me. The security guy even had no clue what I was talking about, and asked me what studio it was in and the name of the person I was suppose to meet.

I'd forgotten to write down the name of the person I was suppose to meet that day and I told the security guard again I was supposed to be here, trust me. But it still wasn't working. So I sat on the curb near the security station, frustrated, and called my agency.

I left a voicemail with my agent and lurked around by the curb until she called me back. I felt like I was in a game of *Monopoly* and couldn't get passed "Go." Damn, the security was tight here. For some reason when my phone finally rang it didn't buzz and I missed her call! Thankfully, my agent left a voicemail and I got all the info I needed to pass "Go" - I was in.

Once inside, a woman around the same age as me, greeted me. She made it seem like she'd been waiting for me all day. But soon enough we walked to the casting room.

In the casting room there was a tall model, and behind her standing on a wooden apple box was a model significantly shorter than her. The smaller model was hiding her body completely behind the taller model and I watched them, and quietly put my bag down.

The smaller model's hands and arms came around the taller model's waist and put a belt around it. Then the smaller model's hands reached up and placed a hat on the taller model's head. Then the smaller model's hands appeared again, wrapping a scarf around the taller model's neck. The taller model stood looking forward, smiling, and made surprised eye movements each time a new accessory was put on her.

Then it was my turn. The other model jumped off the apple box and I jumped on. The taller model stayed. The casting director was glad I watched the previous model and didn't need much explaining.

The casting director had a casual, yet creative spunk about him. He was excited about the project and was hoping to find two petite models with similar colored hands to hire today.

"Just put the hat on her," said the casting director.
"Ok, now wrap the scarf around her neck."
"Loop it a little cleaner, and smoother."
"Do it again."

Then the casting director looked at the storyboard illustrations and asked me to place my hands over the tall model's eyes, then do peek-a-boo with jazz hands.

57

I tried to remember what jazz hands were; maybe it was in the song *"All that Jazz"* in the movie Chicago. It was only a guess. But I didn't want to look ignorant so I said *"Sorry, I could do a lot of other things with my hands, but not jazz hands."*

Just then, another girl walked in the door and watched me fail with jazz hands. The casting directly turned to her and asked if she could do it. *"Of course I can,"* she said confidently.

I started to worry that if it came down to jazz hands, I wasn't going to get this job. Thankfully, being petite, having small hands and my skin-tone were more important. And because our hands looked similar, we both booked the job on the spot.

Then the other model left. She had a full time job and was working in accounting, or whatever.

The casting director asked if I could stay and try on a couple bodysuits. They would be worn for the green screen on the day of the shoot, so that in the commercial you'd only be able to see my hands putting accessories on a few taller featured models.

So I walked with the casting director down the hall to a huge production studio. Equipment was everywhere and builders were working their magic in putting together the set for the commercial. Soon I undressed in a man-made closet area that had accessories and clothing set up on racks and tables. And into the tight bodysuit I went.

Uuugh! It was ugly, super tight. My face was smashed against the bodysuit hood which covered my whole head except for a mesh see through patch, which my eye lashes touched each time I blinked. My nose and ears were totally smashed.

I tried on two bodysuits and each time showed them to the casting director who approved the way they fit. Afterward, I looked totally disheveled. My face looked like I had been out partying all night till 4 a.m. when all I had done was put on tight-ass grasshopper looking bodysuits.

After I got back into my regular clothes, I wondered how the heck I would get back to the city. And I was relieved when the casting director offered one of his production guys to drive me back.

Later that day I received an email that read:

Subject: confirm Thursday for Macy's shoot fitting
fitting tomorrow between 2 and 4.

Tuesday at 2 p.m. was the originally scheduled time for the fitting, but since I had an interview with Sirius XM Book Radio I asked my agent if it was possible to do the fitting Wednesday at 2 p.m. instead. Luckily it was fine.

At the fitting, I was handed a white buttoned up men's dress shirt. I stressed that I needed an XS, or small at the very most, but I was handed a medium. They said don't worry about the size since the sleeves would get hemmed. Also, I was told to bring my own pants the day of the shoot since my hands and arms would be only parts in the shot.

Thursday was the shoot —my third time in Brooklyn this week.

59

To be honest, I really didn't want to wear the bodysuit and the tight hood that I could barely see out of. And it suctioned my head and squished my earlobes. I was quietly glad when the director of the commercial asked the other hand model to get into it and do the *jazz hands* while covering the tall featured model's surprised eyes.

When the hands revealed the taller model's eyes, the camera focused on her *"Oh my God, yay!"* expression. It was very cute. The director was very enthusiastic about the commercial. She was by all of the model's sides, ready to explain something more clearly to get the shot she wanted.

I was asked to put a hat on a male model; I had to place it on his head without covering his eyes. Then the other hand model zipped up a boot that a tall featured model was wearing.

I was watching the tall featured model, who had red hair and freckles, carry a platter of plates and glasses. I was shocked by how well she could keep her balance. I suppose being taller with longer limbs helps.

My job was to take a cup and saucer off her platter when she walked to a certain spot. In editing, they would reverse it to where it would look like the plate was actually being put on the platter. It might sound easy, but there was a timing technique that needed to be precise.

She came from the far left and walked toward the center of the set, while I was on the right. The other hand model was near on the left. We both had to grab a plate or cup, while the tall featured model walked by our hands. Our reach had to be fast, smooth, and pretty...not clumsy and ugly.

We eventually got the shot and it was time to move on to the next scene. This one involved a belt.

One of the tall featured models wearing a belt stood with her waist facing the camera. Then, the other hand model and I worked together, each ready to grab an end of the belt. We unclasped it, and my end went flying back and she held her end.

In edit, when they played it backward it looked like we were quickly putting the belt on the model.

Then it was time for lunch. I sat with the tall featured models. I didn't feel they were prettier than me, just taller. We talked about working with agencies, and the difference between fashion and print and parts modeling. Next I listened to them talk about how their contracts, which were for two to three years, and how that didn't promise that you would book a lot of work. Later they asked me questions about using my body as a model.

They were curious about "that side" of the industry, and soon realized that using your body to model didn't only involve glamour modeling, where petite models are portrayed in a sexual way. I brought them up to speed on how many national and global brands used "full body part models" and that glamour wasn't all the short girl could pursue. I explained that if a shorter girl was ambitious she could find herself modeling for great brands, magazine editorials, and agencies if she knew how to market herself in the direction of commercial print modeling.

And mentioned how I booked this job, *because* I was petite.

So if you think your height is holding your back, or it doesn't have to. Your pint-size self could actually get you the job, and get you ahead.

Subject: HOLD for *Bon Appétit* magazine
Please let me know ASAP if you are avail for this hold

To be honest I am not a die-hard hand model. I think it would be boring as hell if my life was just fingernail polish and cuticles. But working as one has helped me work with great agencies and brands.

~

Today we were shooting a holiday-themed Italian meal. There were three of us today. Six hands that were able to cut the slow-roasted pork and onions, scoop broccoli, and hold glasses of pinot grigio and sangiovese. We were all wearing cream-colored long-sleeve shirts or tan long-sleeve shirts since the photos were going to be in a winter issue.

An eye-catching way to shoot food is from above. The camera is hung in a sturdy ceiling mount and angled down toward the food. It can also be easily be moved and adjusted by the photographer by hand or from the computer. So we just hold our poses. The photographer either gets on a ladder to adjust the camera, or just fires away directly from the computer, to got the right shot.

On the table was a plate of Parmesan and smoky paprika frico, white plates in front of each of us, and a serving tray with an ornate fork on it. The fork had a handle that looked like a twig from a pine tree.

The Parmesan and smoky paprika frico had a burnt caramel color and broke easily in our hands. But that was OK, because the idea for the shot was to make the food and table look as "realistic" as possible....crumbs and a little dishevelment were encouraged.

I placed the tips of my fingers on the white plate in front of me, and then with my right hand I picked up a small piece of the crumbled paprika frico. The male model, across from me, put his fingers around a glass of pinot grigio. The other female hand model, who had a more adult-shaped fingernail than me, placed one hand on the rim of the white plate in front of her.

Soon the roast pork came out, which already looked half-eaten. And pieces of pork were placed on our plates and then panettone panzanella with pancetta and Brussels sprouts were arranged next to the pork. Then sangiovese was poured into our glasses.

The other female hand model held her glass of sangiovese with one hand and rested the other on a mint green napkin. The male model was told to cut the pork with his fork and knife as if he was really about to enjoy a portion of it.

My job was to create some movement for the shot by scooping some broccoli out of the casserole dish. I was supposed to scoop fast enough to create movement but slow enough that it wouldn't look like a massive green blur when the camera clicked.

Next was dessert. It was a delicious apple-cranberry crisp with polenta streusel topping, and vanilla ice cream. The ice cream on my plate was purposely made to look like it was melting next to my apple-cranberry crisp. I let it be, and put a hand on the small handle of my espresso. The other female hand model held her fork and acted as if she was diving happily into her apple-cranberry crisp. The male model casually clenched his napkin.

During a break, one of the food stylists asked if we had any favorite lotions and creams that we used on our hands, and if we could suggest any to her. So I told her that LUSH's Lemony Flutter was my favorite cuticle cream. The other models didn't share anything. Their smiles implied they were secretive about those types of things.

I recall one model at an earlier booking yapping about how another model had done her wrong. Whining, she said, *"...and after I helped her and told her about my favorite salons and everything!"* It was right out of a soap opera. I couldn't help but smirk. Sure, she was a popular hand model and had modeled for many magazines and brands, but it was hard not to think to myself, *"Does she have anything else in her life, but her hands?"* It's funny how some hand models are even protective over where they get their hands manicured.

Despite thinking its funny, hand modeling *has* paid my bills before. And it is an alive industry to this day. Hand models are used for many campaigns – from cell phones, to cosmetics, home goods, accessories, the iPad, and much more. And I, for one, have held a lot of forks, knifes and salad tongs.

Subject: Hand casting today
pharmaceutical ad.

It was a cold winter day, around 20 degrees outside. And there were about three people ahead of me when I got to the casting. I signed in and gave the casting assistant my comp card. She clipped my comp card to my sign-in sheet, and then handed it back to me.

On set, a male hand model was setting his hands the way the photographer asked – by stretching out his arm and showing the camera his palms and then the front of his hands. He was holding something, but I was too far away to make out what it was. The photographer was trying to adjust the little thing being held by the male model, to make it look perfect.

"Let's hide those other fingers," the photographer said.

"Hide my hand!?" the male hand model asked surprised!

"No, just those other fingers," the photographer said.

I took off my brown cardigan, moisturized my fingers, and

67

rubbed a little lotion on my arms and elbows. You never know what will be photographed at a casting. They say hands but it could be your elbow or upper arms in the shot as well.

So I was sitting in my favorite short-sleeve brown dress when I started to get a little cold. They had the window open even though it was freezing outside! I didn't want to be a pain in the ass and ask to shut it, nor did I want to put my cardigan back on since lotion was still soaking into my skin. So, I stood up and walked to the other side of the room where it was warmer. And waited for my turn.

Sitting among the hand models at this casting, I reminded myself that many hand models are not young. I listen to the other models chat about their children, cooking and their recent bookings. A few recognized each other from other jobs. One lady was talking about having to re-order comp cards to change her last name due to her recent divorce.

Then it was my turn.

On set I hold my sign-in sheet with my name and # 12 on it, and smile.

Next I put my hands side by side in front of my face to show them off. Then show the front and back of my hands. He takes a couple shots.

The photographer pulls out a paperclip out from his pocket. I thought to myself that if I had to keep track of a paperclip, I'd probably lose it in five seconds. But of course I don't tell him this.

The photographer asks me to hold the paperclip with two fingers. I get a good grip on it with my thumb and pointer finger so it doesn't go flying across the room or fall in a crack on the floor. Showing it off in a pretty way requires focus. I hold the paperclip steady.

It takes finger balance. It also involves arching the fingers – sort of like arching the body to make them look pretty. I have to keep them looking relaxed at the same time. Too much tension in the fingers can create a red and white color at the tips of the fingers, which isn't attractive to the camera. With all of this on my mind, I hardly breathe while the photographer takes the shots.

We change finger angles about ten times. I can tell the photographer thinks I am young, as he speaks to me in a sweet way while I move my fingers and the paperclip. One thing is for sure, I have the youngest hands in the room, which can be a good thing. Well we'll see soon, if I book this job.

Remember, at a casting, no matter how small or basic the item you are modeling is, treat it like it is something precious and of value. Even if it's just a paperclip. As a model you are really working in the business of advertising and marketing, and these days so many products need a hand to hold them. Why not let it be yours?

69

Subject: Max Factor casting TODAY
Casting specs: hand model, medium-light skin tone

The casting was located just below the Meatpacking District in an eco-friendly and spacious office without walls. The door to the building was open and a cool breeze came through.

There were absolutely no walls in this building besides the outside ones! It was very open. Even the stairway had just a thin wire as a railing. The design of the building was definitely interesting. You could tell creative people work here.

A few feet away I reached the reception desk and said I was there to see so-and-so. The receptionist pointed to the couch. I do as her finger tells me and make my way to the other models. I was glad to see there were only three other girls waiting.

I didn't see the typical sign-in sheet so I asked the girls on the couch who was the last girl who arrived, so I know the order.

I sit and wait for my turn.

71

It's so weird at hand modeling castings because everyone sits there waiting for their turn to show their hands, while staring at each-other's-hands.

A pale blond is sitting next to me, a short-haired tall brunette is sitting next to her, one older curvy Hispanic woman who is obviously going next is waiting by the stairs. I can hear another model upstairs being seen, and there is me.

The blond next to me has long, ladylike fingers. The brunette next to her has hands that aren't even that pretty; mine are small and lean (I wear a size 3.75 ring).

One model has nude nail polish, one has none on, and one has her nails colored maroon. I have a light, light pink. I observe the other models discreetly; we all notice each other but not much is said between us. At hand castings you are not being hired for how stylish you are or how pretty you are. It's about your nails, fingers, knuckles and wrists.

When another model arrives, the reception points to the couch and we make a place for her kindly, but no one talks. Castings are not places for small talk; I mean everyone is competition for the job.

It's like a bunch of horses hanging out in the same barn before the Belmont Stakes, anxious to win. Only for us, we're hoping to win this modeling job.

Sitting on the couch I write in my journal, check my Facebook and Twitter on my phone. Now I'm the one on deck and I stand by the stairs.

The model before me is coming down the stairs and says to me, *"She is in the bathroom but you can go up."* The model is obviously talking about the casting director; I say back, *"OK, thanks,"* with a smile and go up.

When I get to the top no one is there as expected, so I stand next to a wooden table and put my portfolio and comp card on it. And wait.

I smile at a man who is coming up the stairs; maybe he is an art director or something. Then I see a short woman, about my size, talking on her cell phone and walking toward the open space where I am standing. She stands near a large column, which is probably holding up the whole building, and talks about how great the casting is going. She's obviously the casting director, and I try to sense any dishonesty in her voice. Maybe the casting wasn't going well – until I showed up. I play with my hair, adjust my denim dress and just stand there like a patient solider.

When she gets off the phone she asks, *"Did the other girl tell you to come up?"*

"Yes," I replied.

She rolls her eyes *"That's weird, must have been a major miscommunication,"* she huffs, *"I told her that I would come down and get the next girl."*

I smile in an agreeable way and arch my eyebrows to show I know what an idiot the model before me was.

73

Then the casting director asks for my name. I tell her and place my comp card in front of her. She looks at my card but says she isn't taking cards or looking at portfolios and that she just casts on raw photos now.

Damn, I wished she was looking at portfolios because I've arranged mine with all my beautiful hand modeling tear sheets in the front. So I brag, *"I recently did a shoot for Macy's, are you sure you don't want to take a quick look?"* I want her to see how kick ass my portfolio is, but she isn't interested.

I follow the casting director to where she plans to take the casting photos.

As we walked she said, *"I like your shoes."*

And I guess I'm an overly friendly person sometimes because I literally asked her, *"What size are you?"*

She said, *"a six."*

So then I said in a slightly excited tone, *"I'm a six! Do you want to try them on?!"*

I could tell from her unsure smile that she was surprised I asked that, and she said, *"No, it's ok."*

Next, the casting director asked me to place my hand on the nearby white, cement barricade that looks like the wall of a balcony. So I place my hand flat on the cold cement with my fingers together, gently and sweetly. She took a shot like that, and then asked me to hold the can of Pepsi that was sitting on the white cement barricade. At her request, I place the can in the palm of my left hand and let it rest it there. Then, with my right hand, I act as if I was opening the can.

After she gets the shots, I ask if I should tell the other model to come up or if she will go get her. I didn't want to be the idiot model, like the one before me. She smiles and says to tell her to come up now, so I head downstairs.

The next model and *her hands* were already waiting at the bottom of the stairs. She eyed me up and down as I made my way down the staircase. When I reached the bottom I told her, *"You can go up now."*

As I left the casting I was thinking about how models and racehorses are similar in that we are always preparing for our next accomplishment.

Subject: Wednesday Easy Spirit shoot

<u>NOTE</u>: Model should have clean, neutral mani and pedi (i.e. Essie "Ballet Slippers" or similar) and legs should be shaven.

There was no casting for this job. Instead, my agent asked me to FedEx my portfolio up to White Plains, NY. I was living on Wall Street with my boyfriend and it was an easy walk to FedEx Kinko's on Water Street. Sadly, the store is right across the street from where fashion model Ruslana Korshunova jumped to her death.

I hoped my portfolio wouldn't get ruined in the mail or misplaced. There were tear sheets that showed I was becoming an established, professional model which took years to build inside it. Tear sheets that my little self worked so hard to get. Tear sheets that would be a royal pain in the ass to replace. I didn't want to contact all those magazines and ask for back issues. It was a rough to not have my portfolio for that week.

I knew I had the job when my agent wrote me an email to get my address and zip code, because they will have a car pick me up and bring me to White Plains. The email also asked, "*you don't mind sharing with the makeup artist."* Of course I didn't mind. Who would? A car picking me up? Awesome.

The makeup artist's name was within the details for the shoot. I quickly Googled her and learned that she is a pro at eyebrows and loves to shape them. This made me a little nervous. I imagined her staring at my eyebrows, ripping them apart and thinking they were so ugly – massively in need of reshaping. That night I spent an hour tweezing and cleaning up any stray hairs.

~

I typically wouldn't wear heels to a shoe modeling job, to save my feet from pain or any redness. But since it is a job for a shoe company under the Nine West umbrella, Easy Spirit, I decide wear some Nine West heels. Why not? I like to be a part of the team and environment.

I was the first person the car picked up. Then we went to the Lower East Side to pick up the makeup artist. She wasn't in a good mood, or it seemed that way. The moment she plopped down in the seat she starting ranting about the world and what she hated about it. I just wanted to stay positive and I zoned her out. My pedicure looked great, I was about to shoot an ad campaign, and from what I understood I would be the only model. My foot and legs would run the show.

Finally, I saw a big white building in the distance and felt like we were approaching OZ. Good, I couldn't wait for some coffee. However, we couldn't get in since the marketing assistant hasn't arrived yet. I really needed to use the bathroom a well.

After a few tries calling the office, we get buzzed in. There is a huge rack of clothing waiting for me inside the studio room, and the stylist is organizing it.

We do introductions. I meet the photographer, his assistants, the art director, the stylist, and a few other random helpers. It's always kind of weird when everyone greets you, especially when you know all they're interested in is your feet. It makes you feel important, but also a bit self-conscious as they stare at every toenail.

Afterwards, I run to the bathroom. Then I take off my heels and put on my comfy sandals, and become model-ready.

The makeup artist sets up in front of a table with a mirror, and I sit in front of her as she lotions my legs and feet.

I notice that there is a computer near the set, which I like, so that I can see what the shots look like while we are shooting.

Today I will jump up and down in fitness shoes, lie in a manmade sandbox, sit on a fake seawall, and model ten different shoes and a handbag.

Things were going well – the lighting was good, and my foot looked nice in the shoe. I had been sitting on the seawall with my legs crossed. But then the art director and photographer were stumped on the pose for the next shot so I suggested something different. I stood up, leaned my butt against the seawall and put one of my shoes against it, while keeping my other leg down. They liked it.

79

Side note: Models should be perceptive. Most of the time, as the model, you are not involved with the creative process at all. You just need to be natural and quick to understand the shot, —modeling involves a lot of listening. However, when the time is right I think having a creative side can be one of the greatest assets a model can have. It's important to work as a team with the photographer to accomplish a creative shot. Not just being a model that shows up.

At lunch I found out that the photographer wanted to publish a book. I figure everyone does and we talked about publishing for a bit. I joked that I could eat as much as I want as long as it doesn't go to my feet.

Then we started shooting again.

Sand was a big part of this job since the images were for a spring and summer campaign. Lying in the sand, in a flowered sundress and a gold sandal, I felt like I was at a real beach. I angled my legs to make them look longer and the summer sandal looked flirty.

The day was almost done. Soon I'd be able to say that I had shot a whole shoe campaign myself.

During the next weeks, I kept checking the website to see when the images would appear and I ordered myself a few catalogs from the website.

~

It was pretty awesome to see my feet and legs in the large window displays at the Easy Spirit stores and in shoe sections in department stores – even at Macy's in Herald Square. They

80

were seen by millions of people. These images prove once again that a little model can do big things.

(photo: Michael McCabe)

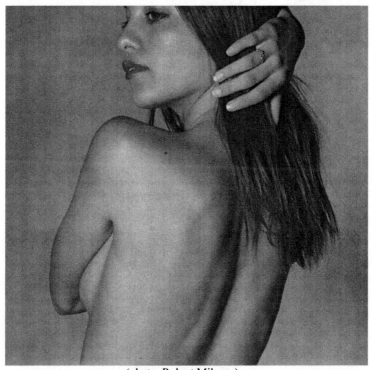

(photo: Robert Milazzo)

(photo: Michael McCabe)

(photo: Robert Milazzo)

(shot by Michael McCabe)

MODELING TIPS FOR SHORT CHICKS

Five Steps to get ahead as a Short Model

"The more you want the more work it involves."
~ Isobella Jade

Modeling as a shorter girl is tough, that's for sure. But I'm a big believer in having belief in yourself and in making things happen for yourself. If you want to work as a model and you are not a tall giraffe, you have to notice the other assets you have that make you marketable as a model. With this in mind here are five tips for getting ahead as a shorter model:

1) Create photos that sell what you've got.

So you're short, so what! I'm sure you have more to offer than just your height and measurements anyway. The modeling industry is much bigger than just fashion these days. Commercial print modeling is a prime area for a shorter girl to pursue because print modeling isn't as judgmental on a model's height. If you know what you can realistically model for, then it is easier to create photos that can better market you.

These are 15 products shorter girls could model:

- Accessories: such as jewelry, handbags, belts, sunglasses, hats, watches and shoes. Shoes are especially important since most magazine editorials, ad campaigns and catalog/online retail sites use shoe models that are a size six or seven shoe.
- Beauty products: such as skin care, hair care, and cosmetics.

- Grooming products: such as shaving products and tweezers.
- Feminine hygiene products: such as tampons and other feminine hygiene products.
- Electronics: including cell phones, computers and head-phones, etc.
- Home goods: such as appliances, furniture and housewares.
- Tights, panty hose, and socks.
- Fitness: including ads, commercials and fitness magazines that show models riding a bike, working out, running, etc.
- Travel: travel magazines, resort ads, airlines ads.
- Pregnancy magazines and maternity wear.
- Glasses and contact lenses.
- Laundry detergent and home goods.
- Book covers.
- Pharmaceutical products.
- Even The United States Postal Service has used print models.
- Pharmaceutical products.

I love fashion. But not all models are fashion models. If you see the modeling industry as just fashion then you miss out on a lot. Focus on how many products need models and take a chance on yourself. Market yourself the right ways, with the right photos. Target yourself with photos that flow with these products to intrigue an agent. Then it is best to create a comp card and submit it to a commercial print modeling agency.

To understand the shots you need to pursue print modeling, you should be aware of the shots you don't need.

- You don't need shots that involve a lot of makeup on your face. Even if you want to model for a beauty and cosmetic ad campaign, you want to focus on a beauty shot that has a natural look, not with heavy cakey makeup. The client wants to see your natural face before they hire you.

- You do not need a high fashion shot or over styled clothing. Instead, flaunt your smile and wear mainstream apparel in your shots. Also, observe lifestyle product ads as a guide for how to pose naturally and be realistically expressive in your photos. Print models are hired for their personalities and approachable looks, clear skin and healthy hair. Print models are hired because their look fits the product's personality as well, which usually involves being friendly or happy and showing expression in a commercial print ad. This has nothing to do with height.

- Skip the glamour shots and avoid overly sexy photos. These shots will turn off a commercial print-modeling agency. If you want to model swimwear or lingerie ensure the photo still shows your spunk and personality in a pretty way. Look at magazine editorials you'd see in *Glamour*, *Marie Claire*, *Cosmo* or *Allure*. And pay attention to what you'd see in a Macy's, JC Penney or Target ads. If in doubt, think health, beauty, and fitness ads when creating a body shot.

- Also you don't need a modeling school.

Although it can be a hustle and a lot of work to get the right photos, get comp cards and a portfolio, and then and mail your comp cards out to agencies, it is the way for a short girl. Typically, most print modeling agencies do not craft your career or mold you into a model. Also, print agencies usually do not have open calls. Submissions are often still by postal mail. Also having a comp card makes you appear more professional and ready for castings and bookings. Working non-exclusively with print agencies is often the lifestyle of a shorter model. Shorter models do not typically find exclusive representation until they are more established, but still can have a lucrative career working non-exclusive.

2) Spend on your goals, invest in your pursuits.
At the start of my modeling career whenever I made money in modeling I always put it right back into my pursuits: creating new comp cards, getting a new portfolio or printing new portfolio prints, and much more. And of course back into beauty and body upkeep as well, like manicures, pedicures and beauty products.

Focus on having the right model marketing tools, such as a comp card. A comp card will get you further than a website or profile modeling hosting site when it comes to working with an agent. And an agent leads to working with real brands and attending real castings. Yes even in this Internet-age, a comp card is your best marketing tool. If you are wondering if you

93

should get a comp card or portfolio first; focus on getting a quality comp card first, your portfolio grows over time.

3) Know yourself and your assets. It doesn't matter if you know the latest trends in fashion or every top model's name and their story by heart, but you do have to have an understanding of your own self when you are not as tall as a giraffe.

The more you know yourself and focus on realistic goals, the better. Make sure you know your assets. If you don't know your assets, you should ask yourself *"what do I have that a brand would like?"* Do you have great eyes, great legs, personality, great skin, great hair, or great energy? These are all assets of a model. Spend time focusing on putting those assets of yours to use as a model – with photos that compliment your assets.

4) Self promotion.
Getting the attention of a modeling agency takes work. It might take more than one comp card submission and mailing to an agency to get in the door. Sometimes it takes improving your comp card and three, four, five, six submissions to the same modeling agency over the course of a few years to hear back! In some instances the reason you're not hearing back from them might not be you, it might be the images on your card. Improve your photos, update your comp cards, and mail them out again, keep trying. You might have to make a couple different comp cards until you have one that works and that an agent likes.

5) Skip the Internet all together.

The Internet is amateur place to start promoting yourself as a model. The majority of what is on the Internet is a waste of time and not professional. An online profile is not considered professional by the professionals. Professional commercial print modeling agencies don't care how many hits or comments your online profile page got. They want to see your professional modeling comp card. The Internet can also be deceiving. Print modeling agencies have websites with directions on how to make a submission to them, but mostly they suggest you submit to the agency in a professional manner, by mailing your comp card to the agency by postal mail. Banking on the Internet to make you a professional model can lead you to getting complacent in amateur-land.

Getting opportunities as a shorter model means discovering your assets beyond your height and marketing those assets. It is possible to work with brands and magazines. But you have to be willing to roll up your sleeves, grab your boot straps and put in the time, energy, and work it takes to be prepared for the opportunity for success.

Focus on the professional, by surrounding yourself with others who are professional, and you will become one.

Six Differences Between a Fashion Model and a Print Model

"Don't let the differences between you and tall giraffe models hold you back."
~Isobella Jade

Fashion Model: Over 5'7"
Short Model: Petite is considered under 5'5" in modeling. However, being under 5'7" is still considered short in the industry.

Fashion Model: Goes to open calls or could be discovered by a model scout from a fashion modeling agency. Or even mails snapshots by snail mail to the agency.
Short Model: A short model should strive to work within commercial print modeling; however commercial print modeling agencies do not hold open calls. Non-fashion models (commercial print models) make their own comp card and mail it to a commercial print modeling agency by snail mail.

Fashion Model: Usually is not booked for a modeling job because of her personality. She might jump, smile, and model products but her photos are more about attitude and less about smiles.
Shorter Model: Her photos are more about personality, and modeling lifestyle products. Her photos are less about mega makeup and styling and more about being natural.

Fashion Model: Gets a portfolio and comp card made for her and the price for these are deducted from her paychecks.
Short Model: Will create her own marketing material, comp

card and portfolio herself. She will use her comp card as a main marketing tool to get a modeling agency. Once you have an agency that wants to work with you, then you give the agency your comp cards to use to market you with. Sometimes a print modeling agency will advise you, and give you tips on making a comp card but you should always have your own marketing tools, your own comp card.

Fashion Model: Typically works exclusively with one agency for a two or three year contract.

Short Model: Typically will freelance and often with a few commercial print modeling agencies or talent agencies. Exclusive representation isn't the end all because in print modeling it is typical to work for years with many agencies non-exclusively. When the shorter model's experience has been established and her portfolio is strong, she might be able to get representation with a more prestige print modeling agency.

Fashion Model: Usually is 16-22 years old, but the supermodels from the 1980s are staging a comeback.

Short Model: There is no age limit for a commercial print model. She can easily model well into her retirement age. Think of Life Alert, hearing aids, BONIVA postmenopausal osteoporosis medicine, etc. Also think of all the ad campaigns showing an extended family, showing a child, parents and grandparents.

It is good to be aware of the differences, but don't let your height hold you back; strive to find opportunities in modeling while using what you naturally do have.

The Scoop on Modeling Marketing Tools

"The more prepared you are for your success, the better."
~Isobella Jade

Unlike a fashion model, you may be surprised to learn that it is normal and expected for a shorter model to produce her own marketing material. This includes creating photos, printing comp cards, buying a portfolio and maybe putting a headshot together as well. Modeling for a shorter girl is very hands-on, and it involves prep work, research, and time. It is best not to rush the process.

What is a modeling comp card? A *composite card*, or a *comp card* or also called *a card*, is printed on an 8.5"x5.5" card stock paper. The modeling comp card shows some of your best photos and includes your measurements/statistics and contact information. It shows a selection of images – sort of like a mini portfolio – that highlight what you can do as a model. On the front you should have a headshot or beauty shot and on the back include two to four images. Typical statistics, or "stats," on the comp card include: height, dress size, bust, waist, hips, hair color, eye color and shoe size.

How do I pick photos for a comp card? Making a comp card is something an aspiring model needs to have a handle on. Mainly it comes down to picking the right photos--photos that will market you in the right way. Your comp card is your best marketing tool; you will use it to get an agent and later to book modeling work so the photos need to be carefully chosen. You need to think about modeling jobs you can realistically get and brands and products you can realistically model for, and shape your comp card around shots that show your energy and personality.

Where do I get a comp card printed? You can print your comp card at a printing studio that specializes in comp cards and headshots. There are also many online printing services. Try www.compcard.com. I also suggest always seeing a physical sample or *proof* that you can hold in your hand, not just see on a computer screen, before you approve the order.

How much are comp cards? Price varies depending on the quality, but you should expect to pay a dollar or two per printed card. A great deal is 100 comp cards for $100.

How many comp cards do I need? For a new model it is all about trial and error. For your first batch of printed comp cards I would order 50-100 and mail them to commercial print modeling agencies in your city as well as magazine photo editors, smaller ad agencies, production companies, etc. I have two different comp cards: a) one for commercial print modeling with photos that express my personality and lifestyle look, and b) a parts card for parts modeling that show my hands, feet, legs, stomach, etc., in an editorial style.

How many comp cards do I mail a modeling agency? Submit only one or two comp cards during your first submission. If the agency is interested they will call and ask for more cards, usually 10-20 cards, which they will use to market you as a model and share with their clients.

What is a modeling portfolio? A modeling portfolio also known as *your book*, is a selection of your best photos and tear sheets placed collectively in a 12.5"x 9.5" portfolio. You will present your modeling portfolio at modeling castings. A standard portfolio is black. And I personally prefer a leather portfolio. I suggest going to an art store or a photography store to find a quality portfolio.

What photos should be in my portfolio? It's a selection of your best photos and tear sheets. And it should show your range as a model.

How do I print modeling portfolio photos? You can print your portfolio photos at a local printing studio or from an online printing service. For online services, I suggest using Adorama.com for digital printing. Also www.compcard.com has portfolio printing. You will want to print your portfolio photos 9"x 11," but ultimately it depends on the size of your portfolio. My portfolio book size is 9.5"x 12.5" and holds 9"x 11" prints nicely.

The Short Model Dictionary Basics

"Knowing the language of the modeling world can make you a better model."
~Isobella Jade

A **modeling agent** works at the modeling agency and represents you as a model and also markets you as a model to their clients. An agent negotiates your booking rate and sends you on modeling castings. An agent is also known as *a booker*.

A **commercial print modeling agency** works with hundreds of models of all types, ages and ethnicities. Their models are booked for print ads, commercials, catalogs, online campaigns and much more for lifestyle products.

A **casting** is like a model audition, or a model interview. The client has let the agency know the description of the type of model they'd like to book for a campaign, magazine editorial, commercial, etc, and the agency sends their best models that fit the description to the casting. A casting can involve 20-100 models showing up unannounced. Usually they are held in photo or casting studios, but sometimes are held at the offices of the brand or at a magazine office. Castings are typically during the day between 9 a.m. and 5 p.m. I encourage you to think twice about attending a casting at night after normal work hours, as professional castings are typically during the work day.

A **go-see** is when the client has already chosen which models they want to see and is expecting you. A go-see casting usually involves the client seeing less models because the client has already narrowed down the models that are desired to be seen. This is also sometimes called a *"request casting."*

A **direct booking** means you got hired based on your photos alone. There wasn't a casting for the modeling job and you didn't meet the casting director or client beforehand.

A **callback** is a second interview or second casting with a client. The client is still deciding on the model, but has chosen a select few to see again before making a final pick.

A **cattle call,** also known as an **open call,** is when many agencies send many girls of a certain type to a casting and 50-100 girls or more are usually seen.

Being **booked** means you have secured a modeling job. What follows are the details of the shoot such as what time to show up and where to go.

A **call time** is what time to show up for a modeling booking.

Sometimes you will have a **fitting** before your modeling booking, where you try on the clothing and accessories that you will be modeling at your booking. This ensures to the client that everything fits properly and certain adjustments can be made before the shoot day.

Being **on-hold** for a modeling job means that there is the potential to be "booked" and the client is highly considering

104

you for the job, but is still deciding on the model. You are not totally booked yet. It means to hold the day, keep it available 100%, until you hear again from your agency confirming the booking or releasing you from the hold.

A tear sheet is the credit or proof that you have gotten exposure in a print publication, magazine, advertising, or catalog as a model. Also it could be online in the form of a product's or retailer's website such as Marshalls.com or Victoriassecret.com. If you do get a modeling job for an online retailer you can copy the image from the web and then in Photoshop adjust the resolution to 300 dpi which is print size. You can also adjust and crop photos at Picnik.com. Or use a PDF converter.

Commercial print modeling sort of is like acting in a photo and it involves real-life situations. For the photography, the model has to often "use" or "hold" a product. Commercial print modeling involves modeling for every day products which are also called *lifestyle products* and services such as banks; a phone company, insurance company; pharmaceutical company, a car company, jewelry, skin care, accessories such as handbags or shoes and sunglasses, fast food chains such as Wendy's and McDonald's, cleaning products, baby products, hospitals, technology products have used models of all types for its commercials print needs. Commercial print models often are every day looking people and are also known as "real life models." Today, many actors are also commercial print models as well.

Editorial modeling is modeling for a magazine. An editorial photo is the photo that goes with an article in a magazine; it's the pictures you see in magazines that are NOT ads. These editorials include the fashion and accessory photo stories you see in magazines like *Glamour, Marie Claire, Shape, Redbook* and *Fitness*.

A **freelance model** works non-exclusive with more than one agency. Imagine you are a writer and you write for a few different publications, this is similar to working as a non-exclusive print model. You work with more than one agency and can freelance with them all at the same time.

A **sign-in sheet** is a sheet that models sign at castings which keeps the models in numerical order of how they were seen. Signing in for a casting involves writing your name, your agency and your agencies phone number on the sheet. Sometimes it involves writing more information such as your ethnicity or measurements as well.

A **model voucher** is an invoice that confirms you did a model booking. A modeling agency will give you this voucher, typically its three pages. After the booking both you and the client signs it. Then you get one of the three pages, the client gets one and the agency. It is your proof, and the agencies proof, you did the job. After a job, I usually fax or mail the agency my voucher so that they can bill the client later. Sometimes the voucher states the usage of the photos that were taken during the booking and the billing information for the client.

A **model release** is a legal document between the model and the client or photographer that states the permissions and usage of the photos from a shoot. Typically the model release is a part of the *model voucher*.

Day rate, half day rate and fees are the amount of money you are making per hour, for the half day or full day for a modeling booking. Your modeling agency negotiates your rate for a booking with the client, which can be based on your experience as a model.

Typically a modeling agent/agency/booker will take 20% of your booking rate from the jobs they have booked you. If your rate for a modeling job is $1000 from a modeling job, then your check from the agency should read $800.

A **headshot** is a photo of your face that starts at the top of your head and can go down to your shoulders. A beauty shot is usually a close-up of your face as well.

A **full-length shot** is a photo of you from head to toe. Many clothing catalogs shoot their models full-length. Full-length can also be while lying down or sitting in a chair as well.

A **three-quarter shot** is from your waist to your face. This shot can also be taken from the head to the mid-thigh or just below the knee and above the ankles.

A **profile shot** is the side angle of your face. Eyes are not to camera and instead the shot is of the side of the face. This is a pretty angle for a beauty shot or a shot involving jewelry.

It's best to keep in mind when cropping your photos to never crop an image at your wrist, knee, ankle, elbow, it can look very unflattering. Your photographer should know this and know how to position and place you in the frame for the shot so you look your best.

4 Photos Every Short Model Needs

"When you focus on what you need you get what you want."
~Isobella Jade

To find modeling opportunities as a short girl it is not just about getting photos, it is about getting "the right photos" that can lead to opportunity.

With the growth of commercial brands the advertising world has also gotten more commercial. This means that more brands are using more models that relate to the consumer and more models of different sizes and shapes are being used in print campaigns and commercials.

This is why it is best for a shorter girl to show that you have a "commercial print" appeal in your photos. And bring forward your smile, energy and personality. Your photos should include showing you can model a product naturally.

When you create photos and your comp card, ask yourself, "What product am I selling in this photo?" and "Why would an agency want to work with this girl?" Often, the difference between a girl who is "working as a model" and one who is just being cute and showing off in photos is that the model has a comp card that she mails to agencies and she aims for professionalism.

No matter your height, commercial print modeling means personality. Skip the fashion poses and the strong diva looks, also avoid overly glamorous shots and intense, stiff poses.

109

Trying too hard, or looking too tough is discouraged. Remember, being natural sells better as a commercial print model. Here are the photos to get:

A headshot with a smile
This should be from the shoulders up. Wear natural makeup, not heavy colors. Hair should not be overdone. You should show a real smile – as if something is funny, or amusing. The photo can be shot inside or outside. To get inspiration check out the models on the hair color boxes in the drugstore; these girls have fresh smiles and a happy-go-lucky appeal.

A beauty shot close up
This can be from the shoulders up, the neck up, or super close. Think of a skin care ad or jewelry ad. The focus is on your facial features. Again, your makeup should not be too heavy. Your eyes should pop but do not go overboard with eye shadow. Use a nice powder or foundation, and your hair should be out of your face. The main idea is to show off your facial features.

A shot that shows your personality and you *doing* something
This shot shows you in action…walking down the street in a cute simple black dress and showing a smile, or walking your dog, holding a handbag, talking on the phone, putting on shoes, washing dishes, holding a bunch of shopping bags, putting on makeup, etc. The goal is to create a shot that shows you *doing* something. Even a shot that shows you typing on a computer would be good these days

110

Before you shoot, think about ads and editorials that involve a story, or something happening in the shot, and apply that to your photos.

Full body shot
A full body shot is from head to toe. The photo could be of you in a bikini, fitness clothing, or a dress. If you choose to show your body, then it is best to pose as though you're in a swimwear catalog or women's health magazine – but don't become a pin-up. If you want to show your shape, it could be in the style of the Victoria's Secret catalog, or wearing a Champion sports bra. It's best to add a smile.

Remember your comp card is yours, there is no strict rule book for laying out the images on the back of your comp card. You could have two shots on the back up to four. You just don't want to clutter the back of card. The front of your card should show a nice headshot or beauty shot. Your eyes should be the center of attention and the first thing the person looking at the photo notices.

Making Legs Look Longer and Posing as a Shorter Model

"Get to know what you're working with and work it!"
~ Isobella Jade

Even if you are five-feet tall, you can still pose your legs to make them look hot and longer! Here are some tips on getting the most out of every inch you've got.

Look in the mirror and get a handle on your proportions
Notice what happens to your body when you move your arm a certain way? What happens to your legs when you position them a different way? Go ahead. Turn your body at different angles and notice what happens. Hold a product while you practice, like a handbag, and pose with it.

Look at magazines and get inspired from the images you see before you get in front of a camera
It is good to learn from observing examples of print modeling before you shoot. Look at magazine editorials and campaigns for lifestyle products, handbags, sunglasses, shoes, even cleaning products, and reenact the pose. Ask yourself, *"What makes the model look great? Are her legs angled a certain way? How is her posture? What are her arms doing?"* Modeling involves thinking, knowing yourself and body, and how to pose it. Whether you are tall or short you should always be aware of your proportions when you shoot.

Always create space between your limbs, especially your legs and arms

Not extreme space, but you will want to create some space between your limbs to give you more length. The closer you hug your body, the bigger you will look. For the upper part of the body, focus on creating slight spaces between the elbows and the body. For the lower part of the body, something as simple as a bend at the knee or keeping one leg closer to the camera can make you appear longer. Arching your back slightly and stretching your neck upward are also important for looking taller. In addition, focus on your posture. When sitting, sit at the edge of the seat and position your legs slightly asymmetrical.

Notice where you distribute your weight
For a shorter girl, the thighs are a major area that can make you feel even shorter in a photo. Try putting all of your weight on the leg furthest from the camera, then casually bend that front leg and arch your back.

Don't try too hard
You still want to be you! Print modeling involves using your personality to model. Feel relaxed, not tense and uncomfortable. The goal in print modeling is not to be a weird contortionist; the goal is look natural and real.

Work with a photographer who knows how to shoot people of all sizes
A professional photographer will; an amateur typically won't. Strive to work with a photographer who knows how to photograph people of all sizes.

I hope these tips help you when you're are in front of the camera.

114

Five Modeling Jobs Where Height Doesn't Matter

"Perception means everything when trying to work as a model. Knowing that modeling is not just for one size or type can lead you to opportunities."
~Isobella Jade

It's true, I'm one of the tiniest working models out there. But even so, I've still worked with great brands and magazines. When I was told I was too short to model, I put what I did have to use and it helped me work with modeling agencies. Here are 5 modeling jobs where height isn't a big thing.

Hand modeling

Hand modeling isn't just about having nice fingers and nails; in fact, I've seen and worked with many hand models that do NOT have flawless hands. We all have imperfections. Who hasn't ever scratched their finger or gotten a paper cut? With that said, hand modeling is perfect for shorter girls who have small hands that are dainty, have thin fingers and nice nail color and nail beds. Size of the nail varies, and hand models are not measured by one standard rule.

To start pursuing a hand modeling career you need professional photos of your hands that show that you can use them to model products. The shot can show you wearing rings and bracelets, holding a wine glass, a cell phone, a cosmetics product, or even placing a bar of soap in the palm of your hand.

Showing expression with your hands is important. It is best to hold a product like you really would use it and do it in a pretty

115

way. Get photos of your fingernails with nail polish, and without.

Hand models are all ages, and ethnicities, and all types of hands are needed and used in the industry of hand models. You might not have the height or measurements for the runway but your hands could allow you to work with some great brands and magazines.

Great skincare item for the hands: LUSH's Lemony Flutter cuticle cream.

Shoe modeling
Getting your foot in the door as a model can literally involve your foot! My first modeling job was shoe modeling. And most shoe models are short, not tall giraffes. A size 6 or 7 shoe is typically liked in the shoe modeling world. Similar to hand modeling you need to target parts modeling agencies that represent shoe models. Having nice feet, toenails, and pretty ankles can mean over a thousand dollars a day and shooting a shoe ad campaign. I've shoe modeled for Brown Shoe, Marshalls, Easy Spirit, Victoria's Secret, and many others. So you need photos of your feet in sandals, heels, boots, sneakers, some without shoes, and with toes painted and not.

When it comes to hands and feet, there are modeling agencies that specialize in *parts* modeling. These are the agencies to target your modeling comp cards to: Parts Models, Body Parts Models Inc, Flaunt Models or CESD for hand and shoe modeling. Start Googling and research "parts modeling agencies" or print agencies that have "parts" diversity.

Great skincare items for the feet: OPI, AVOJUICE lotion.

116

Accessories modeling
No one ever asks how tall the jewelry model is. Modeling earrings, rings, and necklaces is something a girl of any height can do. These days there are many more handbag designers and accessories designers that need models. Think about modeling for scarves, belts, gloves, hats. And they are not just skyscraper tall and are not just on the runway.

Great skincare items for the full body: Alba, Nivea and St. Ives lotions.

Hair modeling
All textures, styles, and colors of hair are welcome. From print campaigns, to hair shows, to product packaging to hair styling editorials in women's lifestyle magazines, they all need hair models. And there are also magazines that specialize in hair and styling. Remember hair modeling could mean modeling hair accessories such as hair ties and curling irons, hair extensions, and hair dye as well.

Create photos that show your hair both in its natural state and styled, similar to a hair product ad.

Great hair care items: before a job or casting try the V05 hot oil treatments, which I love, or John Frieda's Root Awakening conditioner.

Beauty modeling
Put your bright eyes, beautiful lips, and clear complexion to use in modeling for cosmetics and skin care products. High end cosmetic brands often use a taller fashion model for their campaigns; however, there are many, many cosmetic and skin

117

care brands out there from all price points that might consider a shorter model. An aspiring cosmetics brand or growing brand at the mass market level would be best to approach. Also, I suggest attending and noticing the exhibitors at the IBS (International Beauty Show, Ibsnewyork.com). Learn as much as you can about the world of cosmetics and what brands are up and coming! Self promotion is key to working as a model when you are not tall, so grab your bootstraps and get your photos, comp card, and portfolio together and start marketing yourself.

Your skin is an asset that can get you a modeling job, so take care of that skin! Along with my face, feet, hands and legs, I moisturize my neck and chest area, shoulders and back.

Great skincare items for the face: Clinique's Dramatically Different Moisturizing Gel, Clinique's Moisture Surge, and LUSH's Ultralight moisturizer.

Other beauty products to consider: Fresh's Magic Wands Mini Mascara Duo, Bare Escentuals bareMinerals SPF 15 powder, Revlon's ColorStay Ultimate Liquid Lipsticks, Revlon's Extra Curl Eyelash Curler.

Up next is more on what's in the model's handbag.

What's in the Model's Handbag?

"Working as a model involves a lot more than posing and looking pretty; it involves a lot of upkeep."
~ Isobella Jade

Being picture-perfect on set requires a model to take major safety measures. There are gritty behind-the-scenes upkeep and products that help get the job done.

I have all these *holy shit* last minute beauty tricks. I always carry my "model get-it-done-materials" such as a teeny-weeny Noxzema Bikini Shaver, which is small, discreet and perfect for cleaning up little stray crotch hairs or hair anywhere. A dab of foundation or loose powder will cover small hairs along the bikini line just fine as well.

The scar on the side of my knee, from a roller-skating accident when I went crashing into a metal trash can years ago on Riverside Park, can be nearly erased with a mixture of a body lotion and liquid foundation.

I can clean up other areas really quickly too: Before an "eye casting" I know how to make my eyebrows look nice even if I haven't tweezed them in a week by adding a dash of dark brown eye-shadow to carefully cover any stray hairs. A tiny smear of foundation under the brow line makes it all look smooth and clean.

For "hand castings" I can keep my manicure looking nice with my favorite cuticle cream from LUSH on days when there is no time to run to the salon. I even like using my cold face-

119

masks on my feet sometimes. Moisturizing and taking care of my skin is a daily routine.

Weekly I give myself homemade hand and foot scrubs with my morning coffee grinds, it is the best foot scrub ever and your soft body will love you afterward. I save my coffee grinds and use them during my evening shower by mixing the grinds with a body wash for a fantastic coffee scrub. St. Ives Apricot scrub is also great to exfoliate hands and feet. With all of this in my repertoire basically every single day I am ready for the job.

Here are some things I bring to my model bookings and consider go-to-model-items to have in your bag for castings and bookings:

Sandals
Always bring a comfortable pair of sandals or flip-flops to bookings to wear during breaks.

Robe
Sometimes the stylist won't have one for you. So bring your own if possible when a shoot requires a change of wardrobe or jobs that involve the body.

Food and Water
Even if there is catering, you still want to be prepared. Bring water and granola bars to keep your body hydrated and full of energy.

Hairclips, hair pins and elastic hair ties
Sometimes for castings and on the job the client will want your hair out of your face.

Cell phone charger
While you are working you might get called for other jobs or castings to schedule, so keep your phone charged. Though keep it on vibrant or silent while at your booking.

Q-tips
These are some of the handiest modeling tools ever. You can clean up your face, nail polish, and a million other things with a Q-tip.

Thongs
Models need to have their own black, nude colored and white thongs.

Band-Aids
Just in case.

Panty-liners
To put in the undergarment for lingerie, swimwear or body jobs.

A Sharpie and a pen.
To write your agencies phone number on your comp card and to fill out sign-in sheets at castings.

Tampons
Just to be safe.

Lotion
Small travel size lotions to moisturize before castings.

Nail polish
Light colors, silver, pale pink, nude or neutral colors are best to show off your nails. Keep nail polish in your bag for last minute touchups. Once the way to a magazine casting at Hearst I accidently scraped my nail on the cab door and had to quickly fix my nail polish on the go.

Travel size toothbrush and toothpaste.
If you have a casting after lunch or something.

Also keep in mind when you are going to a casting or a booking you are there to do a job. Leave the fight with your boyfriend, or any other emotional moment at the door. And focus on getting the job done as efficiently as possible. In worse case scenarios, it's better to ask where the bathroom is or take a water break than to end up crying in front of the whole crew. You want to appear capable and professional. And the client should feel like they hired the right girl for the job. You!

When you are at a booking remember your drama is not why they hired you. Once I had my period, and I had a job for a shaving company. I had to be basically naked for nine hours. However, I still made sure that no one knew the whole day of shooting that it was my time of the month. Part of being a model is keeping your positive spirit and not letting a challenge or bad day get the best of you, even if it means smiling through your cramps or hiding your tampon string on set.

Tips on Preparing for Modeling Castings and Go-Sees

"Give yourself a chance."
~Isobella Jade

Before you walk into a casting or go-see, it is best to know something about the brand, magazine, or client.

What is the vibe of the brand? What have their previous campaigns looked like? It's smart for a model to know something about the personality of the brand before the casting or go-see, so that you can better prepare to fit the vibe of the brand. Here are some more tips on preparing for castings and go-sees.

What to wear to a casting?
I wear typically jeans, boots or heels, and a tank or t-shirt. However, this depends on the casting or go-see. I try to style my clothing based on the vibe of that casting and product or magazine involved. Sometimes I change into different outfits if I am between different go-sees that have different vibes. I try to dress the part. To look like the girl who could model that product.

Typically for print modeling you are going to go-sees for brands that are not as fashion forward, so you don't have to go into overdrive when it comes to styling yourself. Makeup should be simple, natural and pretty. Don't over-enhance the lips or eyes. Hair should be out of the face for beauty and skincare go-sees, but for other castings use your hair as an asset that goes with your personality. Always bring a hair tie or clip so you can quickly adjust your hair if needed.

123

What does the casting involve?
Before a casting, your agency should give you the breakdown of what the casting involves and what the client is looking for. And if it seems confusing, then ask your agency for a more detailed explanation. If you are unsure of how to hold the product you're going on a casting for, then practice giving a natural pose involving the product. Practice ahead of time doing what the casting might ask you to do: like putting on shoes, smiling, modeling jewelry, holding a cell phone, or whatever the casting might involve.

Customize your portfolio and comp card for the casting.
Arranging your portfolio before a casting is a good idea. For example: if you are going to a casting for a shoe company, put shots of you modeling shoes and your leg shots at the front of your portfolio. So that when the casting director opens your portfolio, they will see photos that fit the vibe of the job that you are hoping to book.

Above all, having confidence, high self-esteem, and the ability to quickly show how well you mesh with the atmosphere and concept of the product or campaign can help you nail the job.

Modeling Casting Etiquette

"The word complaining and modeling do not go together at castings."
~Isobella Jade

Don't sigh

Castings can take a long time, so understand that and don't complain about how long it is taking. This is the life of a model. If you are a brat, asking how much longer the line will be, that is not a professional attitude.

Quiet please. Speak quietly when talking on your phone at a casting, and keep your phone on mute, no one wants to hear your phone ringing or buzzing every five minutes because of a new text message you've received.

Have respect

After you try on or use a product at a casting, put it back the way you found it. Fold the shirt, or put the shoes nicely back on the table. Be a neat model.

Be kind

Always be gracious and kind at castings. Say *"nice to meet you."* and *"thank you."* These little acts of professionalism will be remembered.

Resist to bitch

Bitchy models don't book many jobs. Even if the shoe is ugly, hurts to put on or is too small, act like you love it. Compliment the brand when at the casting. If you are trying on a shoe and it is a bit too big, just walk your best in it. Agree with the editor or brand manager that the shoe is big but also add that *"it's ok, I can do it. I can walk fine in it."*

You want to show you are willing to make it work, that you care about the job, and that you should be hired.

Three Tips for Finding a Photographer

"Value yourself."
~Isobella Jade

The photography for your modeling pursuits is not something to rush. Finding a professional photographer is worth the research and self investment. If you are having trouble finding a photographer consider these tips:

Look in the phonebook

I am serious. It might seem convenient to go to the Internet to search for photographers; however, this doesn't typically lead to a professional result. Remember, most professionals are not on the Internet looking for models to shoot and many social media model sites typically do not feature established professional photographers. Focus on researching professional photographers who have a photography business using a phonebook. Get their names and then use the Internet as a research tool to find more information about them and their photography services. Also strive to find a photographer who works with local magazines, companies, and has a portfolio of work that proves he has been hired by publications – look for tear sheets. You want to strive to work with photographers who are as ambitious as you are, and who also aims for professionalism.

Try a photo school

Many aspiring photo students are learning about the craft of photography and perhaps you can get some decent photos from working with them.

Does the photographer know what print modeling is? And the type of photos that are acceptable for print modeling? If not, don't work with them. You don't want to just shoot to shoot; you want to shoot to get opportunities. The photographer you work with should know about the opportunities for models of all sizes, so that you will be photographed properly.

Invest in yourself
Expecting to get photos for free can actually mean getting nothing of value for your pursuits. Sometimes professional photographers do test shoots with aspiring models; however, always discuss the shoot ahead of time to be sure you are getting photographs that can benefit your pursuits and it is not a waste of time.

Short Model Marketing Tips

"Show professional examples that you can model and you'll have a bigger chance of an agency wanting to work with you."
~Isobella Jade

Your model marketing ability can lead to modeling opportunities. If you know your assets and focus on marketing them to the right agencies, you can find opportunities working with great brands. The difference between someone who wants to do something and someone who actually does it is the *will to try.* Try in the right ways, and with enough confidence, to handle the disappointment and the realities that come with being a model. It is a self-made world. Research and good marketing are major parts of being a short model.

Can you imagine getting yourself in a magazine? Well, it is possible.

Can you imagine approaching a brand and getting modeling experience? You can, and you should.

It is important for an aspiring model, especially a shorter one, to seek out modeling opportunities.

Getting a tear sheet in a magazine can lead a print modeling agency to give you a chance. Your presentation of photos is what is going to interest an agent, or agency, so experience working with an aspiring brand or local magazine can work wonders. So be assertive as a model and don't be afraid to make your own opportunities.

Getting your own modeling work

If you've mailed your comp card to modeling agencies and not heard back, it might not be you. It could be that your photos aren't professional, so put in some time to show that you are capable and that you have some experience. You should consider trying to get some experience as a model by working with aspiring brands and accessories designers, local magazines, boutiques, or fashion students. Also, a print agency doesn't teach you how to model naturally, and modeling schools only focus on fashion…and I'm not a fan of modeling schools in the first place. So you should start with some local action to get some experience that will help you present yourself to an agency in a more professional way. And by showing you have experience, that you have been hired as a model before for an aspiring brand or local magazine can help to get you in the door.

Anywhere there are businesses selling products there is a need for a model. I think to get opportunities as a shorter girl you have to be willing to roll up your sleeves, do the research, put in the work, and market yourself. Here are four ways to strive to get some experience on your own through self promotion and get yourself some legit modeling work that can lead to bigger things.

- Proactively approach a local hair salon or nail salon and see if they need a model for their ads and promo material. Drop off your comp card with the manager or ask if you could mail your comp card to the marketing manager.

130

- Attend a tradeshow or craft show and approach some jewelry or handbag designers. Ask if the designer or owner of the company needs a model, and leave your comp card with your phone number and email. Or take their business card and contact them through email later.
- Many smaller cities have local magazines. Consider mailing your comp card to a photo editor at a local magazine in your town.
- Read the *small business* section of the local newspaper and notice what growing brands are based in your area. Approach them through email or at their store about modeling for them.

While you might not get paid the big bucks for working with small companies, local magazines and events, it is a start. And that start can lead to working with an agency and lead to bigger modeling jobs, despite your height. And if you have pursuits of modeling in another city, it's best to go with experience to give you better chances of success.

Focusing on not just getting exposure, but getting the *"right"* exposure.

Collaborate with professional photographers.
Collaborate with professional photographers that want to gain published work in magazines. In other words, those who are serious about the craft of photography and those who are capable of producing a high value photo shoot. Even if it takes a bit longer to find them, stay true to your goals and focus on achieving a better network.

131

During my early modeling pursuits, I gained a few tear sheets in magazines through photographers that worked with magazines and were ambitious to get published as well. I even helped to scout locations, borrow items from boutiques and aspiring designers for the shoot and do research to submit to the right editors at magazines.

And after I had experience modeling for a magazine, a few aspiring brands, and designers – it was easier to market myself to modeling agencies. Experience is proof you can model, that you have been hired. It takes a very focused and ambitious mindset to get your own opportunities.

At the same time remember to be careful, be honest with yourself, and realistic, and to self promote in the proper ways that will benefit your modeling pursuits.

Overcoming Imperfections in Modeling

"Being a model means that you will be judged and analyzed often, but focus on what is great about you as a model, and ignore the rest."
~Isobella Jade

While growing up, the first unique trait I learned I had was my teeth. In my family, my mother, sister and I all have a gap between our front teeth. My grandmother did as well. In a sense the gap represents my roots. And overtime, I've learned to accept my gap, like it, even call it a trademark of my face. I think it gives me character. And I not only accept it today, over years I have learned how to work with my teeth – to control my teeth – and not let them control me.

But is a gap between your teeth considered an imperfection anyway? Or an overbite? Some people think so. But at the same time you could say there is a new trend of having gapped teeth. Think of Anna Paquin, Lara Stone, Jennifer Hudson, and Amy Winehouses. Or is it a new trend or a trend starting all over again? Think of Lauren Hutton and Jane Birkin. In fact, cosmetic giant Rimmel recently hired Georgia May Jagger (daughter of Mick Jagger) as the face of its new ad campaign. And Chanel signed Vanessa Paradis to be the new face behind Chanel's new line of lipstick, Rouge Coco de Chanel, and for its Coco Cocoon ads. And all of these beautiful ladies have a gap between their front teeth.

Recently on my Youtube video page where I give tips about modeling, there was a comment that beauty models must have perfect teeth. I don't agree.

If your teeth are not bright as the full moon and not perfectly straight you can still model, and even still be a beauty model. Often the model's teeth aren't even seen. Overall, having perfect teeth thing isn't a thing to stress about in modeling. If your teeth aren't perfect, it won't hold you back, not if you're ambitious to bring the best of you forward.

I have come to grips with the fact that my teeth are not perfectly straight and that I have a gap and overbite. I have learned to work with it. I smile with confidence all the time at castings.

Remember, something you think is an imperfection could become your trademark. It's all about perception.

It's OK to be short. But not short-sighted.

"I only know I am short when I stand next to something tall."
~Isobella Jade

I know that it's one thing to be short; and that it's another to be short-sighted. I might not be a tall supermodel strutting her stuff on the catwalk, or posing in high fashion clothing for high fashion magazines – but that's not everything in modeling.

Remember, striving as a modeling isn't about just knowing what you want to model, it is about knowing what you're good for in modeling – knowing where you can realistically find opportunity and chasing it. Make sure you're considering all you COULD DO, not just what you may not be tall enough to do. To be successful as a model it really takes a marketing mindset, a perceptive eye, knowing what is marketable about yourself, and being ambitiously realistic. Notice how I said nothing about height; it just takes enough will to try in the right ways.

I love surprising people and the looks on people's faces when they meet me and ask, *"But you're so short. I thought all models were tall?"*

I usually tell them with some sass in my voice, *"Height isn't everything in modeling when you focus on the other assets you've got."* Not matter your height, aim high, because the higher you aim— truly the more you get!

Isobella Jade

Isobella Jade is an author and one of the tiniest working models based in New York City. Her books so far include her modeling memoir *Almost 5'4"* and a graphic novel called *Model Life: The Journey of a Pint-Size Fashion Warrior*. She is currently writing a fictional teen novel.

You can find her at www.isobelladreams.com or on her blog Petitemodelingtips.blogspot.com.

A note from Isobella Jade

Hearing stories and sharing stories is one of my favorite things to do, and I am delighted to share this collection of on-the-job modeling experiences with you. I wrote this collection as a tribute to beating the odds and as a continuation to my memoir *Almost 5'4"*. I want to give a shout out to some of my favorite people who I love sharing stories with: Todd Harkrider, Isabel White, Lauren Carpenter, Curtis Staub, Jacquelyn Lacroix, Melissa Rodriguez, Colleen Brennan, Vera Melo, Maryam Baik, Ginny VanMarter, Micky Lalchandani, Robert Milazzo, Edward Ash-Milby, Michael McCabe, Alex Kroke, Jack Perry, Luke Gerwe, Jazmin Ruotolo and all the girls who read my blog – who often share their own stories, dreams, and aspirations with me.

SHORT STUFF

CPSIA information can be obtained at www.ICGtesting.com
Printed in the USA
LVOW090713281011

252362LV00005B/105/P